ALBERT SCHWENN'S

Memories of the

WAFFEN-SS

Albert Schwenn *with* Rolf Michaelis

ALBERT SCHWENN'S *Memories of the* WAFFEN-SS

An SS Cavalry Division Veteran Remembers

Schiffer Publishing Ltd®

4880 Lower Valley Road • Atglen, PA 19310

Originally published as,
Als SS-Reiter im Osten ...,
© 2016 by Rolf Michaelis, Berlin, Germany.
Translated from the German by David Johnston

Library of Congress Control Number: 2016960015

Cover & Interior design by Matt Goodman
Type set in Minion & Trade Gothic

ISBN: 978-0-7643-5297-3
Printed in China

Published by Schiffer Publishing, Ltd.
4880 Lower Valley Road
Atglen, PA 19310
Phone: (610) 593-1777; Fax: (610) 593-2002
E-mail: Info@schifferbooks.com
Web: www.schifferbooks.com

Contents

Foreword

When I look back on what has happened since I graduated from school, then I would like to say that while I was not exactly fortunate, I did have a great deal of luck in all that happened. This is true whether it has to do with my wounding at Kharkov in August 1943, or that I was the one chosen to be an instructor from 120 assembled men and never had to see the front again. I was caught up in the middle of events when the Warsaw Uprising broke out in 1944, but my involvement was limited more to patrols and the guarding of our headquarters, although I was officially credited with six close combat days.

From spring to summer 1943, my unit was deployed in the rear area. The partisan war was no soft business, nor was my service in the Pripyat Marshes. If we were shot at we reacted accordingly. As the Russian population was our enemy, to me this was legitimate. I therefore made no secret of this when I was interrogated by the Soviets as a prisoner of war. I couldn't believe that I was initially sentenced to death and then sent to Vorkuta as a war criminal for incidents for which others were responsible. After all it had been war, and I had only followed orders given by my superiors. I was therefore all the more shocked by my former regimental commander Gustav Lombard when I met him again in captivity. He cursed every one of his former subordinates, because of whom he was locked up in the USSR until 1955, for they had done it, not he!

I want my account to show, however, that the will to live is greater than the deepest misery and the worst hopelessness. Despite all disappointments, we last prisoners of war hold our heads high and even laugh, even though we suffered so much. I am one of the very last German prisoners of war, who were not released from the USSR until January 1956.

Albert Schwenn

Preface

I met Albert Schwenn in late 1992. I was conducting research for a book about the cavalry divisions of the *Waffen-SS* and for this reason made contact with the veterans association. The person who was then the managing director of the veterans group made an appeal, and as a result many former participants in the war contacted me.

I subsequently had contact with *Herr* Schwenn until 1998, and in those approximately six years he described his wartime experiences and his ten years and nine months as a prisoner of war on about four-hundred 11.7 x 8.2-inch pages. His emphasis, however, was more on describing his time as a prisoner of war than his service as an SS cavalryman. His service in the Reich Commissariat Ukraine (General-District Zhitomir) from March to July 1943, for which he was ultimately held as a Soviet prisoner of war until 1956, received only peripheral mention. I only learned about this by asking further questions.

Albert Schwenn, who came from a very simple working family, showed himself to be a critical observer and interested conversation partner, who emphasized with pointed pen the enduring human attributes, both positive and negative. In doing so he did not exclude himself.

His memories of (partisan) actions in the rear area, at the front and during the Warsaw Uprising, as well as his unbelievably long period as a prisoner of war, contain so many interesting details that now, after almost twenty-five years, I have decided to edit them for publication.

I have added an appendix containing the history of the 8th SS Cavalry Division "Florian Geyer." It serves as background information to Schwenn's recollections.

Rolf Michaelis
Berlin, April 2016

Chapter 1
Recruit in the SS Cavalry Replacement Battalion in 1942–43

I was born on March 26, 1924, in Swinemünde, and I attended school. In the summer of 1939, I began a three-year apprenticeship at Hans Teske Plumbing, a local company. I must say, however, that I had little enthusiasm for it, for I did not perceive the smell of grout, tar and molten tin as the joy of my work. Nevertheless, for three years I marched into this place with an unfriendly old master and arrogant journeymen and installers. While I was able to carry out my apprenticeship quite professionally, I failed my final theoretical examination with great fanfare. And so I ended my apprenticeship without obtaining my journeyman's certificate. This did not bother me particularly, however, for I only saw my apprenticeship as a way to bridge the time until I could fulfill my childhood dream of becoming an active soldier.

In 1940, an *SS-Totenkopf* recruit *Standarte* (regiment) trained on the island of Wollin. I saw the SS men as they marched smartly through the streets and saluted with raised arms instead of lifting a hand to the brim of their cap. That was to my taste and I decided that it was only the SS for me. The same summer I took my physical examination and was placed in Replacement Reserve I category, after which I volunteered. Approximately fifty young men were examined and just eight were accepted into the *Waffen-SS*. None of the others met the high acceptance standards still in use at that time. There you go, that was something! I was part of it and signed up for four years.

My father Wilhelm Schwenn was an unskilled worker. He had delivered beer for the Schultheiß Brewery, and hauled railroad ties to the yard of the Rütgerswerke AG. It was a wood impregnation company. Its main customers were the German Railroad and the national post office. Both had a standing requirement for impregnated wood: the railroad creosote-treated ties for its tracks and the post office and several energy producers impregnated poles for transmission lines. The factory had a National Railroad siding, on which timbers to be treated were delivered almost weekly. The timbers were initially piled in a huge storage area and then impregnated in batches. They were transported by special tipper trucks to a 130-foot-long pressure vessel, where they were soaked in creosote and impregnated under pressure. Then they were dried in a storage area. They were shipped out again by rail.

My father became ill with tuberculosis in 1940 and afterward he did light duties as a maid of all work for the company. Then in 1941, he joined the *Kriegsmarine* (navy) as a security guard. We were given an official residence and father, a service dog and pistol. It was my father's dream to see his son strutting through Swinemünde in coveralls. The people would stop, point their fingers at me and call: "Look, it's Wilhelm Schwenn's boy." No, this wish was his alone!

I took advantage of father coming down with TB in 1940–41 to avoid the obligatory service in the Hitler Youth. Although it was also strictly organized along military lines, I had no interest in it. I said that I had to go to work because my father was ill. First I was an errand boy in a Zimmermann bakery and later for the Werche Delicatessen.

As there was no future in this, and I was still waiting to be called up, in the summer of 1942, I found myself sitting with my father before the desk of two officials in the employment office. I was completely ignored, and they spoke to my father as if he were an inmate in a labor camp. Then he lost his temper and objected. The end of the song was that I was asked quite pleasantly if I would like to start as an assistant fitter at the Ostswine Naval Depot.

I slaved away there for just a few weeks, for soon my call-up from the *Waffen-SS* clanked through the letter box of my parent's home. When the long-desired induction order came, my disappointment was great. They wanted me in the cavalry—me, who wanted to join the tanks or the motorcycles. Though I was terribly disappointed, my father was very excited, for he loved everything about horses and could not imagine the difference between civilian and military riding.

At any rate, I set off by train from Swinemünde via Berlin to the SS Cavalry Replacement Battalion in Warsaw. After changing trains a number of times, on October 22, 1942, I found myself at the Stadium Barracks at the age of eighteen and a half. I was issued an identity disc with the number:

234 – SS Cavalry Replacement Battalion.

My mailing address was:
SS-Reiter Albert Schwenn
Machine gun Replacement Troop/
SS Cavalry Replacement Battalion
Kielce, Radom District – Stadium Barracks

My machine gun replacement troop had experienced non-commissioned officers, but the same could not be said of my *Stabsscharführer* (first sergeant). Not only we recruits, but also the non-commissioned officers complained about our *Stabsscharführer*'s incompetence. Our troop commander at Kielce, an *SS-Hauptsturmführer* Wegener, was also a rather curious superior. He liked to make himself up and his sons had to address him as *Hauptsturmführer* instead of daddy or papa. He lived with his wife, bag and baggage, in an extravagant villa about six-tenths a mile from the Stadium Barracks. It was guarded by two sentries day and night. His neighbor was the battalion veterinarian, with whom he had fabulous booze-up parties at least twice a week. To ensure their success, food was taken from the troop kitchen's larder and the first sergeant let it happen! Wegener's mount was a magnificent white horse with the name Prince, however he was never the animal's master.

Our platoon leader, *SS-Untersturmführer* Riecke, had come from the Hitler Youth officer corps. He loved to signal with his hand: "Non-commissioned officers to me!" and to proclaim: "Spit and polish, the old Prussian way."

Riecke could have been used on any recruiting poster for the *Waffen-SS*. Outwardly and in part inwardly, he had a disastrous resemblance to our first commanding officer Hermann Fegelein. But his splendid appearance was combined with a character that was just as unpleasant. He was bursting with arrogance and pride.

I joined the SS Cavalry Replacement Battalion on October 22, 1942.

The inevitable happened and in fact it was no surprise to us recruits.

Several days before Christmas 1942, *SS-Untersturmführer* Riecke and the 1st Platoon's first section (they were all ethnic Germans, while we, the second section, were all Reich Germans) marched into the training area for practical instruction on hand grenades. He arrogantly played around with a hand grenade, which suddenly exploded in the circle of comrades. It wounded several recruits, one of whom later died. Riecke's right leg was riddled with fragments and he lost several fingers of his right hand.

We buried our comrade in the Kielce cemetery between Christmas and New Years, fired three honor salutes and prayed that we would soon be free of Riecke. He never came back to us. We were then commanded by an *SS-Standartenoberjunker* Schaper. He was a splendid man, tall, a little rangy, and he had clearly grown up in a Christian home. He had probably once sat around a Pathfinder or *Wandervögel* campfire and sung hiking or folk songs. After hours he came to our room and talked or sang with us. Our squad leader *SS-Unterscharführer* Jathe had also remained human. When taps were played at 2200 he opened the door to our room a crack, his suntanned forehead visible under the rim of his helmet, and softly but sharply whispered: "Everyone in bed? All washed? Pitcher filled with water? Good night." "Good night *Unterscharführer*."

With our veterinarian constantly delivering our rations to the troop commander, we complained about our lack of supply. What they were doing to us young recruits in the Machine gun Replacement Troops was a miserable business. Nothing would change, however, as long as we stayed in Warsaw.

We were hungry from the beginning to the end of our time as recruits, and we stole turnips from the supply dump and ate them raw. We went to the service club in the city and bought sandwiches, on which low-fat curd was spread, by the ton. This angered our first sergeant: what would the other units think of us? They probably didn't have a veterinarian giving away their food, and had a top sergeant who was able to stand his ground.

We did have one superior whom we admired, however: *SS-Sturmscharführer* (master sergeant) König, the *Sturmkönig*, our ram, who was to teach us to ride. He came from Baden and in build and appearance resembled Count Felix Luckner, the legendary sea devil. Broad as a farmhouse cupboard, the ram stood in the middle of the riding track, the lunging whip in his right hand, his left paw tucked in his belt. He stood there with his legs apart and scrutinized us from the corners of his eyes as we casually rode in a circle. Then a devilish grin slid over his pirate's face. None of us paid any particular notice, the horses putting one front foot in front of the other, their eyes half closed, like their riders happy about the relative quiet.

The ram raised his whip and cracked it over the smooth hind quarters of a horse trotting by at a leisurely pace. The poor animal

Cavalry training with the SS Cavalry Replacement Battalion in Warsaw.

wakened abruptly from his half-sleep and reared up and raced in panic from the line into the inner track. Then our ram rose to his full height: "So, tell me you monkey, who ordered you to ride out of the line, well? What? Say something you rogue! Hey, are we in the Sarrasani Circus here? Or in the wild west with the cowboys?" The affected rider brought his horse back into the line of other riders. There was still a trace of a devilish smile on the face of our *Sturmkönig*. Satisfied, he cracked his whip again, this time in the sand of the riding track. The "monkey" had somewhat mastered the situation, which was more attributable to the horse having experienced such attention before.

But we young cavalrymen loved him, our ram. A hard man with a soft core. When we left for the front he said goodbye to every one of us, and he said to us: "Make sure you don't try to play the hero for me, lad. Or would you rather not see your girl and your parents again?"

On January 30, 1943, in Kielce city hall, there was a concert featuring the army and RAD (Reich Labor Service) bands and the SS cavalry trumpeter corps to mark the tenth anniversary of the NSDAP's seizure of power. We were the last to march in, proudly wearing our long cavalry coats, the silver runes on the right collar, the SS eagle emblem on our left sleeves and shiny, jingling spurs. How proud we were: "Everyone said, everyone felt: the SS cavalry is charming." It was a wonderful scene when the troop had formed up, the First Platoon with its bays, the Second with its sorrels and the Third with its blacks. But how much trouble and work lay behind it all!

Chapter 2
SS Cavalry Division, 1943

5./SS-Reiter-Regiment 1

After about three months of training, in February 1943, we were assigned to the field unit. We proceeded on foot—panniers bouncing along at the rear—from the Tarschinska School through the entire city across the bridge over the Vistula to Praha, where we were loaded into cattle trucks.

We arrived at a town in the central sector called Yarzevo. It lay almost halfway between Smolensk and Vyazma. Among the units there was 5th Troop, 1st SS Cavalry Regiment. The regiment's commander was *SS-Standartenführer* Lombard. The troop leader was *SS-Obersturmführer* Südekum, a quiet, level-headed man without airs. At his side was the best *Stabsscharführer* I was ever to meet, Rudi Rath. He was a top sergeant from the picture book: incorruptible, strict but fair. He kept his eye on everything, even worried about dirty feet, and he ensured that the vets and cooks saw to the troop's physical well-being. No enlisted man and no non-commissioned officer was safe from him. He acted mercilessly with biting irony if something was up. He once blasted a man who had just been promoted to *SS-Unterscharführer* when, three days after receiving his stripes, he went to the hospital. In this case, however, his action was unjustified, for the bawler Hermann Hasse was actually sick. He had contracted typhus during a bout of drinking with a platoon leader, *SS-Hauptscharführer* Stiehler of the 1st Platoon, in a Russian hut. No one was upset to see this unpleasant and stupid fellow disappear from the scene. I was not to meet him again until the Vorkuta prisoner of war camp.

Our 5th Troop and actually the entire SS Cavalry Division was made up largely of ethnic Germans. There was scarcely a corner of eastern and southern Europe that was not represented within our ranks. There were two lads hanging around the 5th Platoon who

My regimental commander, *SS-Standartenführer* Gustav Lombard, in 1943.

were supposed to have lived as Germans in Russia. Ironically one was called Amann and the other Zucker. Both understood scarcely a word of German and traipsed along behind everyone. We were thus not short of ethnic Germans of every category and one must say, without wanting to offend our comrades, that they were employed mainly within the mounted battalions. The majority of them, those over twenty-five years of age, had served in the Serbian military or had been soldiers in Hungary and Rumania. They had thus served in armies in which the officer was everything and the man—including non-commissioned officers—was nothing. Men were still slapped and beaten regularly there. The older ones had told the young ones, and one day these boys stood in astonishment before a serious-looking but secretly grinning non-commissioned officer. There was no beating here. They stood at attention and looked staunchly at their superior, and this pleased the instructors from the Reich—at last their stripes and silver braid were being showed the proper respect.

I ended up in the 2nd Platoon, which was commanded by *Feldwebel* Heinze. There was obviously such a shortage of senior NCOs by the beginning of 1943, that members of the army were already being seconded (to the *Waffen-SS*). My machine gun commander was an ethnic German from Rumania by the name of Derner. He had obviously served in the Rumanian army, for he already had the rank of *SS-Rottenführer* (*Obergefreiter*) and was soon promoted to *SS-Unterscharführer* (*Unteroffizier*). He did not distinguish himself by any particularly high standard. His favorite saying was: "Do you know what you are? You are a violin, an ass violin." [*Translator's note*: ass violin is a literal translation of "Arschgeige," a mildly derogatory term used mostly in friendly settings and roughly equivalent to the English "dipstick."]

Our heavy troop consisted of two platoons with Model 34 heavy machine guns and one platoon with 81.4 mm mortars. A machine gun crew consisted of eight men and ten horses:

1. Gun commander .... 1 horse
2. Gun commander's horse-holder .... 1 horse
3. 1st Gunner (machine gunner)......................... 1 horse
4. 2nd Gunner (carriage)................................ 1 horse
5. 3rd Gunner (ammunition) .... 1 horse
6. 4th Gunner (ammunition)............................. 1 horse
7. Pack Horse Leader (pack saddle for the MG) ....2 horses
8. Pack Horse Leader (pack saddle for the carriage) ....2 horses

The SS Cavalry Division reached the Eastern Front in March 1943. Training continued near the front in Siberian cold.

On dismounting for combat, the gun commander and machine gunner gave their horses to the horse-holder and the 2nd, 3rd and 4th gunners left theirs with the pack horse leaders. The 1st and 2nd gunners removed the gun and the carriage from the pack saddles, the 3rd and 4th gunners unstrapped the ammunition boxes from the side parts of the pack saddles and followed the gun crew into position. That's how it was planned and that's how it was done.

Shortly thereafter we were transferred to Bobruisk, about 235 miles away. The units of the SS Cavalry Division, which had been rushed to the crumbling front during the winter and had fought very costly battles, was supposed to be rehabilitated there. Our realistic combat training also began there. We lay on the ground behind our heavy machine guns and carried out target and aiming practice with the optical sighting mechanism. Then our regimental commander, who we called "Papa" Lombard because of the quiet, fatherly manner he exuded, appeared. Accompanied by his dog as always, he got down behind each machine gun and peeked expertly through the telescopic sight. Then he got up and said to my platoon leader *Feldwebel* Heinze: "Make this man 1st Gunner." So I became a first gunner on the heavy machine gun. Soon after, *Feldwebel* Heinze was replaced by an *SS-Oberscharführer* who had previously served as an interpreter at *Führer* Headquarters. His name was Zeno Alberti and he came from someplace on the Italian border. He had communicated with the Italians at receptions. Commanding a heavy machine gun was undoubtedly beyond his ability, but he didn't play the wild man and tried to fit in.

The horses we were given stood in draughty barns with no wooden floors. Their coats looked bad, as if they were infested by moths. They were sent to the military hospital for horses for an initial checkup, later they were treated with a germ-killing gas at a veterinary station. We fed them well, which took care of the rest, and before long we were again mounted on satisfactory animals with slick, shiny coats. My horse's name was Peter and he was a pleasant creature. My nineteenth birthday was on March 22, 1943, and it passed rather sadly. My unit took no notice of it and at some point I received a crushed package from home. The only good wishes were from my squad and a few men from my platoon.

Action in Reich Commissariat Ukraine

After the division had been rehabilitated for about three months and we received our realistic combat training, on May 10, 1943, we began a four-week action in the Reich Commissariat Ukraine (General District Zhitomir). Our division commander *SS-Brigadeführer* Fegelein issued a snappy division order which was read aloud to all of us. In it he incited us to mercilessly combat the partisans and the population that supported them. The actions that followed were exactly that. We gave them short shrift. Fegelein had just returned to the division. After establishing the SS cavalry, he had risen to become Hitler's *Waffen-SS* liaison officer. Now he had relieved *SS-Oberführer* Freitag, who had obviously displayed insufficient élan.

We first moved to Lapichi near Osipovichi (approximately forty-five miles northwest of Bobruisk). There we spent fourteen days in a former Soviet cavalry barracks and were used on security missions and to gather agricultural products and cattle. Finally we marched into the so-called Wet Triangle located about seventy-five miles to the south. There, between the Pripyat and Dniepr Rivers, there were supposed to be more than 10,000 partisans, who had taken control of the population and constantly carried out ambushes against our supply lines. It was an area of almost 3,860 square miles, which was virtually under Soviet control.

We got up at four in the morning, rode out by five at the latest, stayed on horseback for two miles and then led our horses for three miles, as they had to be spared. Our regiment's motorized units (for example the 20 mm flak or signals people) overtook us by nine. They sat in their Kfz 15s, leaning back comfortably, and waved patronizingly to us grooms with our horses.

For four weeks we swept the area from north to south. On horseback, we were ordered from village to village and patrolled the area with and without horses in the search for partisans. When we moved into a village (often such villages consisted of just ten to twelve houses) we first called out the village elder, and then the residents were brought from their houses to a central location. While their papers were checked, the huts and sheds were searched to find if they contained partisan weapons or equipment.

If weapons or the like were found, the order was usually given to burn the village and seize all of the livestock. Once I asked my

My regimental commander *SS-Standartenführer* Gustav Lombard.

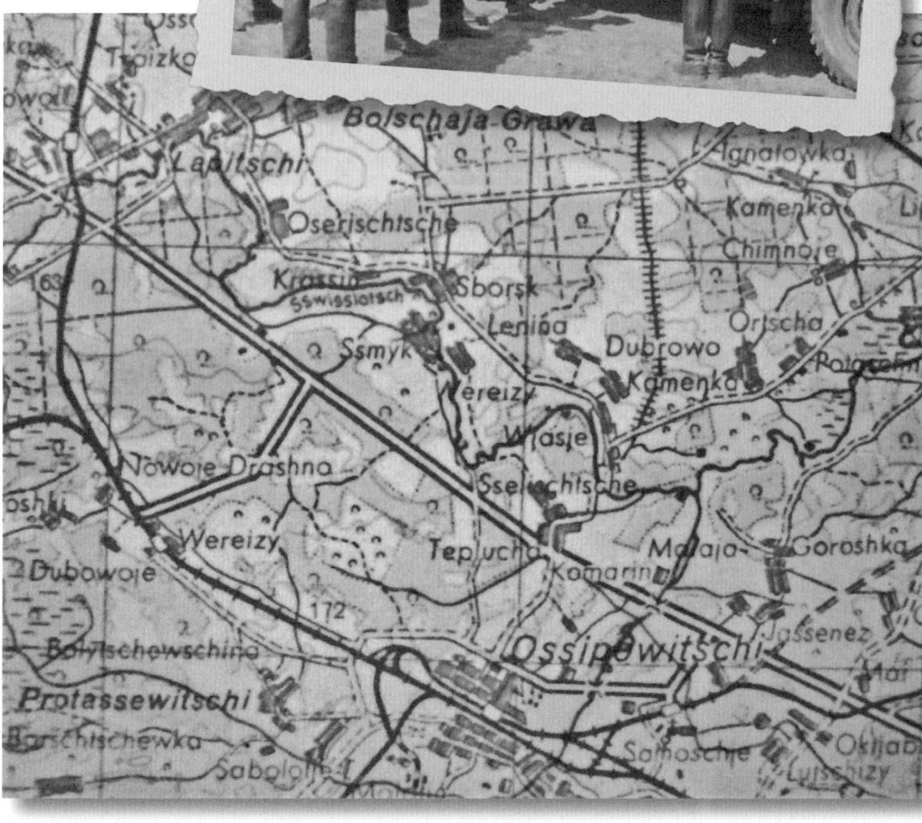

Army map of the Lapichi–Osipovichi area.

The action in the "Wet Triangle."

troop leader Südekum what actually became of the livestock, and he answered "it all goes to Germany." As we ourselves were not suffering from hunger, it may be said that they simply wanted to deprive the partisans of food, for they lived off the land exactly as we did.

The presence of younger men in the villages was always suspicious. Normally all of those capable of serving had been called up by the Red Army, making it quite likely that they were partisans. If these were unable to produce valid documents identifying them as residents of the village, and if our superiors assumed that they were partisans, the necessary orders were issued. In some cases the executions comprised the entire population of the village if they were viewed as suspected partisans; at the very least they were deported to Germany to work.

Many villages were empty when we arrived, although just before there had still been people wandering about. They were terrified. Surely many felt caught between a rock and a hard place. The communist partisans were not exactly restrained in their dealings with the population either. The partisans themselves lived in the most inaccessible areas—in some cases with sympathetic civilians who had fled their villages. We often tried to cross swampy areas on foot ... a practically hopeless undertaking ... if one sank to one's knees in the mud or water, the boots stayed behind. One time a comrade suddenly had solid ground under his feet. What had happened? The partisans laid boards in the morass which helped them get around. Following the path, we came to an island in the middle of the swamp on which the partisans had stored supplies and equipment. In contrast, forest camps were easier to reach ... sometimes the population betrayed their location out of fear. The forest camps usually consisted of wooden quarters that were sunk in the ground like bunkers. Larger camps had kitchens, hospitals, stables, etc. The approaches to the camps were often guarded by mines and camouflaged. They usually began to the side of a road behind bushes.

In the four weeks of "Operation Vistula I" we were shot at from the forests as we made our reconnaissance rides. The partisans after all had cover there. We were never sure if they were traps. Perhaps they wanted to lure us into the forest and destroy us there. We returned fire and reported by radio where we were and that we were under fire. A combined attack on the wooded area was made by the next day at the latest.

Once we came under fire from a village. As the situation seemed clear, we immediately attacked. We with our heavy machine guns were posted on both flanks and soon the first tracers were flying in the direction of the village. The cavalry troops prepared to take the village. It was already a scene of panic. Cows bawled, horses galloped around and numerous figures ran in the direction of the nearby forest. I sent over several more bursts from my heavy machine gun and then followed the assault on the dump. There were already a number of civilians lying dead … partisans or normal civilians, how was one to know? Marks on the ground showed that there had probably also been wounded, who had been dragged into the forest by the partisans. The remaining population was completely terrified as to what was now to happen to them. They loudly voiced their distress and cursed the partisans, who would not leave them alone. We looked tensely at our superiors. It seemed unlikely that this village was friendly towards the partisans, as they had taken their wounded with them. When their papers were checked they were found to be in order. We moved out and the village was not burned down. That, too, sometimes happened.

As we continued our advance we found numerous abandoned partisan supply dumps as well as vehicles and equipment. They retreated before us. If we found a camp, we were very careful, for booby traps were often left behind in vehicles or bunkers.

It began to rain and it eventually became a downpour. Forward progress became very difficult and of course our attention as to what was ten feet to our right and ten feet to our left naturally diminished. The partisans stayed in their hiding places and we simply shuffled along past them. In the marshy, swampy terrain, which was difficult to negotiate under any circumstances, we clung to each other for more support. If we had reached our objective of the day, we waited in that line until dawn came. The only shelter we had was our shelter halves … Completely soaked, we carried on. Only now and then did we receive hot food, as the food carriers seldom made it out and back. And so we were left with our cold rations, which were not exactly palatable. Our camp was painstakingly guarded at night … Pairs of sentries were relieved every two hours.

One night partisans tried to break through our encirclement, which was slowly tightening around them. The shout of, "alarm, alarm!" was followed almost immediately by the firing of signal flares. We got up and immediately manned our weapons. In the flickering light of the star shells, not far away we saw a group of a hundred or more partisans running through the forest. I loosed off several belts from my heavy machine gun in their direction, and my comrades also fired their weapons at the partisans. We saw many fall after being hit. A cavalry troop received the order to attack—we shifted our fire to the right to prevent the enemy from fleeing in that direction. They were also placed under fire from the other direction and the entire group was destroyed.

They lay there, young and old, men and women, some in civilian clothes and some wearing pieces of Red Army uniforms or German or Hungarian tunics and trousers and boots. Their equipment was on the ground and we collected everything … We kept the bread and other food, the rest—including maps—we turned over to the SD (security police).

This, my first action, ended after about four weeks. We returned to our starting positions and were given several days rest. Although we had experienced much effort and hardship, we still played tricks on other units. One day we mounted our "mustangs" without saddles, only blankets and belly straps. The weather was good and we horsemen, with Zeno Alberti in the lead, were wearing only bathing trunks. We put on our belts with our P.38 pistols and rode along the forest road like cowboys, screeching and shouting. We passed through our supply train's resting place. They had tied their horses to the trees, left and right. We scared the devil out of our hard-working supply train comrades. When the last of us was already far away, an outburst of shooting broke out behind us. They looked for those who had played this joke for a long time.

On June 21, 1943, we celebrated the summer solstice. Our 5th Troop was quartered in a tiny village in the Pripyat Marshes. The machine gun teams sat around campfires, drank liquor and beer and smoked and ate, while harmonicas and accordions played folk songs.

At the end of June 1943, we were moved via Mozyr into the Petrikov area west of the Pripyat. "Operation Vistula II" also lasted about four weeks. We advanced south along the Ubort River, driving partisans and partisan sympathizers towards other German units holding the line Olevsk–Ovruch. Unfortunately it again began to rain. Perhaps this was a climactic characteristic of this region, after all it consisted mainly of swamps and moors. If it had been dry all the time, would they perhaps have dried up?

And so we covered ourselves with our shelter halves and rode through the rain. We were constantly accompanied by mosquitoes whether on foot or horseback. As these might carry malaria (swamp fever), we were issued mosquito nets, which we placed over our forage caps or steel helmets, and if I remember correctly also a cream to rub on our hands. Whether one was bitten or not, the mosquitoes were a terrible annoyance. They were with us virtually twenty-four hours a day. The only thing that really helped was the smoke from campfires. I immersed myself in it, hoping that the tiny creatures would leave me in peace. This proved to be wishful thinking, for I was bitten, and six months later I also came down with swamp fever.

At least 10,000 partisans were said to be carrying out their nefarious deeds in the new area of operations. Although it was part of White Russia, the area south of the Pripyat belonged to the General Commissariat Ukraine. Quite a few Ukrainians lived there and most had exhibited little sympathy for communism. Many Ukrainians instead supported nationalist partisans, and they were of much less concern to us than the Soviet ones. The houses of the Ukrainian population were also always whitewashed and clean. This was quite different from the Russian ones we had come to know. There, in winter even the chickens and sheep lived within the four walls with the people.

The Ukrainians often supplemented our rations. They frequently gave us scrambled eggs and pastries without being asked. While an incredible quantity of cattle had been requisitioned from the farmers during the first action in the Wet Triangle, I can no longer recall if the same happened during "Operation Vistula II," however there was no total requisitioning to deprive the partisans of them.

One day I developed pressure pain in the sole of my right foot. My wet riding boots had probably caused a pressure sore to break out and it hurt like hell to walk. I limped to the SDG (medical service aid station) and they kept me there. For fourteen days I drove the

Action in the Pripyat Marshes.

medic's panye wagon with his medical kit and helped him treat comrades and also Ukrainian civilians.

Our action ended in the formation of a pocket filled with Soviet partisans. By then they had lost most of their equipment, and with no help from the population they were also exhausted. We often came upon smaller and larger groups, most of which were then destroyed in combat. We no longer made an effort to determine if they were active partisans or partisan sympathizers or helpers. We didn't encounter much opposition. I don't know of any fatal casualties in my troop and I also cannot remember if there were even any wounded.

Afterwards we stood guard while the Ukrainian farmers harvested their grain and rode with them into the fields. Then we simply sat beneath a tree and enjoyed God's blessings.

Unfortunately this too ended one day and we were moved again. As was so often the case we did not know exactly where, but it filtered through that we were going to the front. I cannot remember that this resulted in an outbreak of euphoria among us. Older comrades had told us how hard the fighting at the front was, and our SS Cavalry Division had not exactly been designed to fight against enemy armored units. I even believe that the SS cavalry had originally been conceived to combat partisans in the remote areas of the Soviet Union.

When we had to entrain at the end of July 1943, we first had to wait for a company of the Hungarian *Honved* to disembark the freight train. I stood on the platform and looked and marveled. There was shouting in Hungarian—"*Hol wan*?" (where is?) and "*Mid wan* ... " (you have ...), and the things that were unloaded from the cars: window frames with and without panes, wooden carvings, umbrellas, piano stools and rusty bathtubs. Unbelievable, I had never seen anything like it. The Rumanians beat their muschik (Russian peasants) and the Hungarians stole like the mercenaries in the Thirty Year's War. Troop commander *SS-Obersturmführer* Südekum stood beside me and, grinning, he said to me: "Astonished Schwenn?" I replied, "I am really astonished *Obersturmführer*. It's incredible!" "Yes, yes," said my commanding officer, "those are our allies!"

Action at the Front Near Kharkov

Our 5th (Heavy) Troop was at its war strength. That meant that we had a total of four heavy machine gun squads (two platoons) and a mortar platoon. We were all loaded into the empty freight cars and transported to the front near Kharkov about 400 miles to the southeast.

When we arrived there about days later, we were unloaded in open country. There was no station nearby and so we procured hay bales from a collective farm some distance away and from them made an unloading platform. Everything went very smoothly. The horses were happy to have solid ground under their hooves again.

Then we moved further forward on horseback. After a few miles we arrived at our destination. Happily, once again everything in the village was very clean and roomy. The houses were whitewashed inside and out, and there were green cucumbers in the potato clamps. We bedded our horses down in the stables and as it was still warm as summer we spent the nights in the open.

We also received a new platoon leader. In the evening we stood in a semicircle around the *SS-Untersturmführer* and he gave a short speech. There was no fanatical enthusiasm for the Führer in his words. "We are now moving into the main line of resistance and we shall fight bravely. Long live our Fatherland!" We shouldered our equipment and under cover of darkness marched forward into the Merefa area, where the main line of resistance was.

When it became light we saw that we had dug in behind an embankment. From there we overlooked the area around us. The Russians were just a few hundred yards away, in a wood beyond a field. Our machine gun position was laid out in the shape of a horseshoe, so that the gun could be pivoted to all sides. At first all was quiet. The first sergeant sent his train people forward and we got hot food, bread, butter, sausage and everything in quantity. Toward evening there was rumbling beyond the forest. The Russians sent us a night blessing in the form of mortar rounds and a half dozen shells from medium field artillery, however all of them fell far behind us.

The employment of heavy machine guns and mortars right in the main line of resistance was not in keeping with theory, as these supporting weapons were actually supposed to be positioned somewhat to the rear. But obviously we lacked the soldiers needed to man the main line of resistance. All of the third and fourth gunners were employed as infantry. They were to the left and right in foxholes, far away from the heavy machine guns. Our troop took over the sector, which would normally have been held by a battalion. Food was again brought up in the evening and was plentiful as always. Our first sergeant was great. Huddled together in our hole, my second gunner Franz and I slept.

The next morning the sun shone down on us beautifully. We observed in the direction of the enemy, nothing moved there. Our side was also quiet. Tragically our new platoon leader went into the wheat field in front of us to better observe the enemy. A shot was fired, obviously by a Soviet sniper, and our *SS-Untersturmführer* died a hero's death *"for Führer, Volk and Fatherland."* When we recovered him, we found that the bullet had entered just beneath his wound badge. We had lost our platoon leader. And now? Who led us now? Where was the troop command post? Where was *SS-Obersturmführer* Südekum?

When we saw an American Jeep with a limbered mortar approaching in a gully, we opened fire. Perhaps the Soviet commander only wanted to know where his enemy was. In response to our fire the Russians blanketed us with medium and heavy artillery. It boomed and howled and shells fell to our left and right and behind us. Then the firing stopped. The neighboring gun's Number 3 gunner had been killed. Nothing further happened that second day at the front. The August sun appeared, and despite the powder smoke and gun oil it smelled like warm earth and fresh hay. Our food carriers came again. Curiously none of us had the need to urinate or relieve ourselves. Washing was all but impossible and the beard stubble slowly grew from our chins.

The next day the Russians began pounding us terribly with their artillery as soon as it got light. It was impossible even to stick the tip of one's nose out of the hole. I heard comrades screaming to my right, during a break in the firing I saw that several foxholes had been flattened, bodies lay about, farther down the firing line had been torn open. Then there was a droning from the sky. I looked into the sky behind me and saw a flight of three Il-2 aircraft, red stars on their wings and tails. Suddenly flames spurted from their wings, and bullets struck the sand behind me and to my right and left. "Man," I thought, "they're shooting at you!" I dove headfirst into my machine gun position.

Then my second gunner jumped from our position. Franzl was an ethnic German and an undoubted genius at organization, cooking and butchery, but after four months of training and two months of follow-up training he had still not learned how to strip and reassemble the machine gun. But now, under the heaviest artillery fire, Franzl recovered a wounded comrade from the wheat field in front of us. I thought he was crazy, but he simply said: "Now what would I say if mother asked, Franzl why didn't you save your comrade?"

Soon after, about six T-34s rolled towards us. Their guns fired and the Il-2s dropped several bombs. There was a terrible crashing and fountains rose high in the sky. They circled over us unhindered, and our 20 mm flak had not the slightest chance of shooting down one of these birds. The Il-2 was too well armored. We abandoned the railway embankment and suddenly I was alone. Where was my second gunner? Where were the others from my platoon and the troop?

I ran to the rear like an orphan child. I had left the carriage and had only taken the machine gun, two spare barrels and two belts of ammunition, 100 rounds altogether. It smelled of powder smoke and burning rubber. I reached two of our 150-mm field howitzers. Their solid rubber tires were smoking and dead gunners lay on the ground. Several unwounded comrades sat there in despair, cradling their heads in their hands. Wounded dragged themselves to the aid station for treatment.

I was nineteen years and five months old and felt completely abandoned. I came upon a heavy machine gun carriage in a shallow depression. I set up my machine gun and mounted the optical sighting mechanism. Up there, that's where the front must be, that's where they would come from ... and that's what happened. Through the crosshairs of the sighting mechanism I saw them coming, their peaked caps with the Soviet star on their heads. Their blankets strapped over their chest, shoulder and back, they appeared beside and behind shocks of wheat. I opened fire and swung the machine gun from left to right and from right to left. Several of the helmets disappeared from the sight and never reappeared. I was shooting

My barely one week of frontline action as first gunner on an MG 34 heavy machine gun took place in August 1943.

as a "one-man machine gun," no second, third and fourth gunners. Then I realized that I was all alone there. Suddenly I thought: "Get out of here, or else it will be your ass. What do you plan to do against the attacking enemy if there is no one else firing with you?"

I removed my machine gun and continued toward the rear. An unfamiliar *SS-Untersturmführer* finally assumed command. I didn't know him, but I allowed myself to be assigned to a position with several comrades. It was getting dark and so I didn't realize that he had put us in a forward slope position. I was lying in a shallow depression and when it began to get light I saw our predicament. We might as well have been on a serving tray. Suddenly there was a loud clanking, rumbling and rattling behind us. A German assault gun appeared over the crest of the slope, fired its 75 mm gun at the suspected enemy positions and drove ahead far enough to cover our withdrawal.

I separated myself from the group and looked for my people. Then I found our supply train, where everything still appeared to be normal. Suddenly the Soviet artillery began firing. The shells burst damned close. I took cover. Lying behind a huge pile of cucumbers, I began nibbling on them, less out of hunger than nervousness. A short time later—tired, unshaven and stinking of powder smoke, sweat and gun oil—I stood beside a barn and stuffed a slice of bread with butter into my mouth. My machine gun was leaning against the wall, when a Kfz 15 drove past the forecourt. Standing beside the driver was our regimental commander *SS-Standartenführer* Lombard. Once in Yarzevo he had made me first gunner. "Come with me boy, I want so see what's happening up front. You have a machine gun don't you?" "Yes *Standartenführer*." "Well then, climb in behind!"

I slung the machine gun over my shoulder and grasped the bipod with my left hand and the grip with my right. My thumb was next to the safety lever. We drove over the railway embankment into a half-harvested wheat field. At some point the driver stopped. Lombard stood up in the front seat, raised his binoculars to his eyes and calmly observed what was happening on the other side of the field at the edge of the wood. Not a shot was fired at first, then however it hissed and moaned around us. An entire salvo from a "Stalin Organ" (Soviet rocket launcher) landed in the field to our right and left and behind us. That didn't bother us too much, however, for while these projectiles made a lot of noise, their fragmentation effect was minimal.

"Back!" *SS-Standartenführer* Lombard had seen enough. We drove back, over the railway embankment, then down a narrow footpath that followed a narrow wood, not 165 feet wide. When we reached the wood, Lombard smiled at me: "You did well son, now get out and return to your comrades. Good luck." Papa was a jokester. Were my comrades even still alive? And if so, where were they? Where was my troop leader, where was my gun commander, where would we get a new platoon leader?

Then some officer or non-commissioned officer who was buzzing about assembled all the men. I was one of them and soon after I was squatting in a foxhole. The nearest comrade to my right was at least 100 yards away, and I didn't see any to my left. The Russians attacked again and we got out of there with our heavy machine gun as quickly as we could. The enemy artillery blanketed us and swarms of Red Army troops advanced. Night fell, now and then there was a bright flash. Somewhere a mortar was active, or a field howitzer, but otherwise the front was quiet.

The fourth day in the main line of resistance began. I spent the night in an abandoned foxhole. Our supply system at least was still functioning smoothly. I stuffed my rations bag with bread, sausage and tobacco products. Somewhere comrades were lying in foxholes, depressions, behind low hills, where the front ran. Suddenly my gun commander Derner appeared! Where had he come from? Derner was probably full of adrenalin. After he fired his submachine gun at the edge of the forest, he took my machine gun and loosed off an entire belt of fifty rounds into the trees in front of us. He did so standing upright with no cover. There was no sign of the enemy. There was no doubt, Derner didn't want to go home to his cow village in the Batschka with just his *Unterscharführer* braid. He also wanted the Iron Cross, Second Class. He was never to return home, however. Comrades at the Convalescent Troop in Warsaw later told me that he had been killed a day after I was wounded.

The dead lay everywhere. One was scarcely recognizable. A hit had ripped open his ammunition box and obviously set off the shells.

The entire body was torn open and his face unrecognizable. That was war. This comrade lay there, and over there another, there lay two SS men, and farther right a complete gun crew dead in their positions.

At intervals the Russians sent us musical greetings with their "Stalin Organs." His field artillery thundered and I heard the flop-flop-flop-flop of the mortars. We had assault guns, but where were they? I only saw the same one driving around and a well-camouflaged battery of 20 mm anti-aircraft guns.

Then an unusual quiet returned to the main line of resistance. While I was thinking, the assault gun curved along the edge of the forest. An *SS-Hauptscharführer* popped out of the hatch: "Well soldier, have they forgotten you? You have a machine gun too. Why not stay with us a while." He was a fine chap. On his black panzer tunic were the Iron Cross, First Class, the Tank Battle Badge, Wound Badge and the Order of the Frozen Flesh. He was happy: "We've been needing a machine gunner!" I couldn't have cared less who wanted me, finally someone had given me a clear order. As well, it was an assault gun, which wasn't much different than a battle tank. That's where I had originally wanted to be. I loved my horse, but I would gladly have given him up for a place in an assault gun. We smoked, the crew climbed in. I squatted behind the entry hatch and placed my machine gun in the slot. I had three belts with a total of 150 rounds hung round my neck.

The assault guns rumbled over the railway embankment, rolled into the depression, through rye fields and stopped. Then the 75 mm gun barked, four times, five times, six times, and I fired a belt into the terrain. Then we rolled back, across the railway embankment into the wood. We climbed out, leaned against the assault gun's side skirts and smoked. To my joy I recognized three comrades walking towards us. I ran to meet them and they were too were overjoyed. They clapped me on the shoulder so hard they almost hurt me: "Albert, you're still alive?" We exchanged information on who had been killed, who was wounded and where this and that man were.

Wounded

One of them gave me a pack of twelve Juno cigarettes. Another was happy that I relieved him of a holder for two barrels. He no longer had a machine gun. But they too had no idea where they were and were wandering around without a squad leader, without a platoon leader. We talked and were happy that we were still alive.

Then I heard "crack." There were two puffs of smoke above the gravel of the railway embankment, then something struck my right arm, which was holding the twin barrel holder. I dropped it, and blood spurted out from beneath the sleeve of my camouflage blouse. My comrades looked at me and said: "Albert, what's happened?" At first there was no pain, just a slight shock. Then I began screaming: "Medic … medic!" I began running, away from my comrades, past the men of the assault guns, who were staring in shock, out onto the road. I instinctively turned left and ran, I was bleeding, but not as heavily as I feared: "Medic – medic – medic!"

"Come here, quick!" At the side of the road, under a bush, lay Heino, our medic. He was an *SS-Unterscharführer* from Berlin. Heino treated me and dressed my wound with a first-aid packet. A fragment had struck me an inch above my right wrist. The legendary "crash-bang" had almost got me. A short barrel, but a long shell case, a high muzzle velocity (V0), the impact got there before the sound of the gun firing, thus "crash" (impact) then "bang" (firing).

"Go down there, the medical clearing station is about two miles. Good luck Albert!" I set off, not wanting to waste a second getting away from there. I walked at the side of the road and after about a mile I heard a motorcycle-sidecar coming behind me. In the sidecar was my troop leader Südekum: "My God Schwenn, have you been wounded?" "Yes, Obersturmführer, I have to get to the clearing station!" He had me get in behind him and we drove about another mile, then I was there. We couldn't miss the standard with the Red Cross. "You'll be healthy again soon and come back to the troop. You were my last first gunner!" That's the shape our proud 5th Troop was in!

Before I knew it there was a wounded slip with name, rank, unit and nature of wound hanging from my tunic. Ten minutes after my arrival I was sitting in front of the ambulance beside the driver. It was getting dark, and in the rear there were four seriously wounded.

We drove across a railway embankment. To the right there were flashes, the Russian was beginning his offensive. His artillery was preparing the assault. Shells from the Russian heavy field artillery howled over us and the gravel of the embankment crunched beneath the wheels. Then we drove up to a large barn, which had been set up as an aid station.

Eager medics first laid me on a stretcher, but this became boring and I sat down on a chair. A medic with the rank of *SS-Hauptscharführer* greeted me like a long-lost brother, told terribly dirty jokes and gave me a tetanus injection in my right thigh. I was transported out and after an hour we came to a very gloomy-looking house. We walked into a dimly-lit room on the first floor in which there were simple bunk beds. We spent the night there and the next day boarded a comfortable military bus. The weather was excellent and we arrived at a farm with a modern building. In the large vestibule sitting at a table there was a *Feldwebel*, who took my pay book. I was told to go upstairs and report to one of the doctors.

A doctor examined my wound, then he handed me to a Ukrainian sister who carefully washed my right hand. Men lay on mattresses everywhere. I spoke to a member of the *Wehrmacht* who was standing there: "Damn," he said, "you can wait here until you turn black. I've been here four days already. They get the badly wounded out first." But that wasn't the answer I was hoping for. I went outside to a field kitchen, which was smoking in a corner of the yard. Soldiers ambled about, some were playing cards. I didn't know how to play skat nor was I hungry. I just wanted out of there, out of cursed Russia.

Then a bus pulled into the yard. I walked over to it. An *Obergefreiter* asked: "Where are the twenty-four men for transport? I have to go, the train leaves in twenty minutes." The *Feldwebel* from the medical section merely shouted: "Let's go, who wants to go with him?" Fabulous, I really was a lucky child. I had been wounded less than twenty-four hours ago, but I was already on my way home. That was in Kremenchug. In the afternoon we arrived at the main station in Kiev. They took us to the delousing facility, which in military parlance was called the disinfestation institution.

An ambulance took me up to the Kiev citadel to an air force hospital. I undressed and hung my clothes, which stank after the delousing, on the hooks, above which there was a card. On it were my rank and the name and number of my wound. Bullet fracture of the right forearm. A young medical NCO examined my wound and the twisted joint. He asked me to give him my hand. I did so and he turned it, causing me a great deal of pain, but my hand was in the right position again. They put on a cast which reached to my elbow.

Every opportunity to transport a wounded man to a hospital in the homeland was exploited. I went on a train transporting Ukrainian SS volunteers. They were on their way to a Polish garrison. Their concern for me was most touching. Using sacks and blankets, they made me a luxurious berth and brought me food and drink. The train steamed into the Cracow freight depot on the second day.

I and the other wounded were taken to Koberczin military hospital. A steady stream of ambulances departed. A *Hauptmann* said to me: "You (three other SS men, lying on stretchers, had been unloaded with me) will be picked up immediately by your SS hospital. They're loading over there where the hospital train is. So don't worry, all will be well." Then he was gone. I squatted beside my comrades and we smoked cigarettes. It began to get dark. The freight yard was quiet and empty. The hospital train sat there, dark and visibly uninvolved. Clean, elegant all-metal express train cars. Finally an SS ambulance came. I spoke to the older *SS-Unterscharführer*. "Everything is fine lad," he said. "Your comrades will be loaded as soon as my vehicle's empty." We were under way about fifteen minutes later and then arrived at the Koberczin SS hospital near Cracow. It had been a mental hospital and there were still Catholic nuns working there.

Then there was a bed, with snow-white sheets. How long since I had lain in such a bed? It was the night of October 20–21, 1942. That was ten months ago. The station medical officer, a *Wehrmacht Stabsarzt*, came to visit. The *Waffen-SS* had not exactly been adequately provided with doctors. I was fitted with a Stuka—a splint that was supposed to immobilize my arm.

My stay there was also a short one. We went to another delousing facility, scarcely fifteen minutes from the station. After the so-called disinfestation procedure we marched to a hospital train. I took my place in a seating compartment and we subsequently arrived in Liegnitz. The train stopped and we got off. In the station forecourt there were Red Cross field kitchens. Female auxiliaries were ladling out thick noodle soup with beef. An officer walked around and assigned the wounded to the hospitals. He came to us—I was sitting with eleven other SS men. "Where do you want to go?" asked the *Hauptmann*. "There are twelve spaces open in Greiffenberg."

I mistook Greiffenberg in Lower Saxony with Greifenhagen in Pomerania, which I knew, and therefore immediately agreed. Anyway, we did not regret being sent to Birkenhof Reserve Hospital there. Greiffenberg was about 45 miles from Liegnitz as the crow flies and we arrived there after a 90 minute drive in an open truck.

There were four of us in a room. Two were from the *Wehrmacht* and two from the *Waffen-SS*. My comrade was Heinz Spremberg of the *SS-Division "Das Reich."* He joked "that's good enough for me." A *Feldwebel* Michaelis looked after everything except for the treatment rooms. *Feldwebel* Michaelis was a hospital top sergeant who had seen and done it all, but he had made sure that everything was done according to the book. Everything ran smoothly.

One day I received a letter from my mother: "We will arrive at 1530, please reserve rooms for three persons." From 1500 I waited on the platform. The trains came and went again, but neither mother nor father got off nor did a third person, whoever that might have been. Evening was already approaching. Half the Reichsbahn had stopped here, then finally a train came from the opposite direction. Father, mother and Aunt Minna got off. "Of course" they had gone past Greiffenberg and almost ended up in Liegnitz. Incredible, three grown people and they couldn't even manage an uncomplicated rail route. I had found my way to Berlin and from there to Warsaw and had never gone beyond Ducherow on the train before. But the autumn there in the foothills of the Riesen Mountains. The days that followed were happy ones.

Reassured and knowing that their son was in the best hands, mother, father and auntie departed. They were plowing the fields on the hills for winter wheat. They called it "German Unity" there. Pulling the plough was a horse, a cow or an ox. I stood and marveled. I had never seen this up in Pomerania, but we didn't have steep hills like that to master.

One fine morning *Oberstabsarzt* Dr. Reichelt, the hospital's chief doctor, who had previously paid us little attention, came and gave

My father and I during my parents' visit to the Greiffenberg Reserve Hospital in Silesia in autumn 1943.

A photo of me as an *SS-Sturmmann* and assistant instructor with the 2nd (Bicycle Reconnaissance Training) Troop of the SS Cavalry Replacement Battalion in Warsaw.

me and my comrade Spremberg each a bag. In it was a Wound Badge in Black. He said nothing and disappeared immediately. I wondered, would the entry in my pay book be made in the hospital or not until later at the replacement unit in Warsaw? I received no award certificate or the like. But Heinz and I immediately scratched the decoration so that it would appear that we were veteran fighters.

But there too, the day came when we had to leave. *Oberstabsarzt* Dr. Reichelt discharged me even though my wound was still festering. November was still in its early days, the sun shone, Peter spoiled us. We proceeded by rail through Neu-Bentschen into the *Generalgouvernement*. The train had to stop and my car was decoupled. The axles were overheating. Some patriot had probably put sand in the oil glands. One look into the barn-like waiting room was enough. I preferred to sit on a bench on the platform, and I placed my field bag next to me, all my possessions. A train pulled in on the next track. On it were female workers. They called and waved and invited me to go with them, they would provide the entertainment. An old soldier beside me said: "Let the women buzz, boy, if you want to get back to your unit healthy and in one piece. They'll fuck you to death, I know from my own experience, my dear chap."

Chapter 3
SS Cavalry Training and Replacement Battalion 1943–44

After arriving in Warsaw I took public transportation to my replacement unit. In the afternoon I reported to the convalescent troop orderly office. Once again I encountered an efficient organization. With the routing slip in my hand, I passed through all the specified rooms. Finally I was quartered in Room 8.

Then I returned to the orderly room and was given convalescent and recovery leave until December 1943. My leave at home was pleasant. I finally saw my girlfriend again and we strolled to cafes together. But there too the day of my return approached and I had to go back to the convalescent troop. Soon after my return, however, the swamp fever I had probably caught in the Pripyat Marshes returned and I was transferred to Hospital 6. Otto Köster, the medical sergeant, was from Stettin and was thus a countryman of mine. Though I recovered, he was able to carry me forward as not yet fit for active service and so I played the role of assistant medic in the hospital for two months. I brought meals to those who were confined to bed and kept their temperature charts. This pleasant time also came to an end, and in March 1944 I had to report back to my unit.

Once again fit for active service, I was assigned to a trained replacement troop. With a strength of about 300 men, it was supposed to leave for the field unit. By then it had been designated *8. SS-Kavallerie-Division "Florian Geyer"* (8th SS Cavalry Division "Florian Geyer"). There an *SS-Hauptsturmführer* appeared before us assembled "mannequins"—he needed six men to serve as instructors and functionaries. His name was Braun Stein and he was commander of the 2nd (Bicycle-Reconnaissance-Training) Troop, SS Cavalry Replacement Battalion. He walked through the ranks and selected his lads. Fortunately, I was one of them (I had risen to the rank of

SS-Sturmmann (*Gefreiter*) on January 30, 1944) and the following day I was appointed assistant instructor of new recruits. I was supposed to help give the boys practical training before they were sent to the 8th SS Reconnaissance Battalion at the front. In charge was a capable senior NCO, *SS-Hauptscharführer* Hölz from Hof in Bavaria, an intelligent first sergeant who was always present.

There was no cleaning out nostrils or tending to hooves with a hoof pick in the Bicycle Reconnaissance Training Troop. The bicycle didn't whinny nor did it kick. It also didn't bite and stayed as clean as it was when one parked it. Some of the newcomers, the recruits of March 1944, were probably surprised. Some had brought shiny spurs with them in their luggage which could not have been of less use in a bicycle troop.

SS-Hauptscharführer Heike, a dozen non-commissioned officers and assistant instructors (including me) marched onto the troop's asphalt parade square looking important, serious and frightening, ogled expectantly and curiously by 120 newly-uniformed young lads. There they stood, our new comrades. Eighteen months before, not far from this square, I had stood on another square and a dashing *SS-Unterscharführer* and an even more dashing *SS-Sturmmann* called Tanker had danced around in front of me and my comrades and had impressed us all mightily. Now I was standing there and was likewise gazed at in complete wonder.

The 2nd (Bicycle Reconnaissance Training) Troop was organized into platoons with light and heavy machine guns and one platoon with medium mortars. IV (Heavy) Platoon was led by *SS-Obersturmführer* Leipheim. Of course he selected the strongest and most intelligent-looking men for his unit. Nevertheless, a few particularly clever recruits dropped out after a field exercise. Allegedly they had tire trouble. Their tired and hungry comrades looked for them for hours and later that night they received a sound thrashing. After that, nothing like that ever happened again!

The troop had hard duty, carrying out night marches and field exercises with map and compass, orientation marches by squad, machine gun firing, and lessons in the use of 81.4 mm mortar and explosives. Often, however, things did go as envisaged with the one- and three-kilo charges. During an underwater demonstration in a pond on the grounds of an abandoned disposal site, three one-

From March 1944 I functioned as an assistant instructor with the 2nd (Bicycle Reconnaissance Training) Troop of the SS Cavalry Replacement Battalion.

kilo charges went into the water followed by one three-kilo charge. Not one of them went off. A fourth one-kilo charge finally put an end to it, and with a respectable column of water bicycle rims, pots, rusty bed springs and other former household effects flew into the air. An enameled chamber pot was later found on the balcony of a house on the road to Gora Calvarias.

The weeks passed with a certain monotony. Then our boys went off to the front. About twenty-five officer and non-commissioned officer candidates stayed behind to take part in a preparatory course we were giving. While I had messed up the journeyman's examination of my plumber's course in a blaze of glory, I was obviously a born soldier. Now, not only was I training others, I was also learning a mass of theory. I had to take part in our troop's non-commissioned officer course that followed, and I achieved the best marks.

There were signs of unrest in the Polish capital however. They sent us no more recruits. We more or less bummed around. We were attached to police units and took part in heavily-armed patrols through the entire city. One day our mess NCO was shot at from a passing truck while in the middle of the street. He was fortunate and suffered only a grazing wound in the calf.

We solemnly celebrated Hitler's birthday on April 20, 1944. There was a parade with flags, standards and companies from the army, air force and *Waffen-SS*. On June 21, 1944, I leapt over a campfire on the parade square of the Moronic school to celebrate the summer solstice, shouting: "Better dead than Slav!" Then came July 20, 1944: "A very small clique of ambitious, unscrupulous and at the same time unreasonable and criminally-stupid officers have devised a plot" and attempted to assassinate our Führer. I do not remember how I reacted then, but we were immediately placed on alert. We were loaded into trucks and the 2nd Troop rolled to the assembly point at the Ulan Barrack, with our IV Platoon with its heavy machine guns and mortars leading the way in Schwimmwagen and motorcycle-sidecars. Warsaw was filled with replacement training units of the *Waffen-SS*. Were we now to fire on our comrades of the *Wehrmacht*? Fortunately it did not come to that. But it was remarkable how quickly even incompletely-trained units became battle ready.

Training young recruits on the 81.4 mm medium mortar.

Training young recruits on the 81.4 mm medium mortar.

Training young recruits on the MG 34 heavy machine gun.

As the Red Army was at the gates of Warsaw, our SS Cavalry Replacement Battalion was moved to Training Camp Bohemia. Only clean-up detachments remained behind, of which I was a part.

The Warsaw Uprising

Our battalion commander *SS-Sturmbannführer* Plänk and the battalion headquarters had also stayed behind and they were in the former embassy buildings in Warsaw opposite the Copernicus Observatory and Belvedere Palace. *SS-Unterscharführer* Hans Miebs and I, along with others, were assigned to guard the headquarters buildings.

The situation in Warsaw changed more and more. Something was in the air. Fewer people showed themselves on the streets. There was a terrible smell. On August 1, 1944, Hans Miebs and I were sitting by the window in our quarters, chatting. Then we saw an astonishing sight. Our comrade at the sentry box darted forward and took cover behind the old cannon at the entrance. Then he began shooting with his submachine gun. This amazed and amused me in equal parts, but that didn't last long. Hans too had looked outside and quickly realized what was happening. "Quick, take cover Albert. They're shooting at us!" And that was precisely what was happening. Bullets smacked into the wall of the corridor and knocked plaster from the ceiling. As we were the guard, we had the weapons with which to defend ourselves.

I took a machine gun and began firing belt after belt at the attackers. There was firing all over the place. Alert units were quickly formed from people who were picked up everywhere. They included some who had only ever worked in headquarters with pencils and sharpeners. As active soldiers, we were also sent on reconnaissance patrols. Our mission was to determine if the surrounding streets and blocks of houses were free of the enemy.

Once we searched apartments in the vicinity. We were on the third floor of a very stylish apartment house and even looked under the beds. Then we heard voices down below in front of the house and then feet crunched on glass from broken windows that littered the pavement. I cautiously stuck my head out the window and below saw about a dozen members of the Polish Home Army, who were probably also not feeling too brave. After fifteen minutes they disappeared and we returned in relief to our quarters.

We had meanwhile been moved into the rooms in the cellar and we sprawled on elegant couches and easy chairs. We smoked luxury class cigarettes and drank spirits we had found in one of the apartments. During our missions we pocketed an unbelievable quantity of things from the apartments and prisoners.

We selected about thirty people from a group of captured civilians to dig a communications trench from our cellar entrance to the front garden of the observatory. The foundation wall was broken through, and an underground tunnel was dug beneath the front garden, sidewalk, boulevard and riding path. This enabled us to go from where we slept directly to the bunker under the ten-foot -high iron fence without being seen. The bunker was roomy and had a raised standing place for the machine gunners. Also in the bunker were two easy chairs and a smoking table. One day the Red Army began a fierce artillery bombardment. When it was over, we in the bunker were deaf and our hands were shaking.

Later when we stumbled back into our cellar in the headquarters building, we found six older men there wearing party uniforms. "There he is! Schwenn, I've been looking for you for a long time. Gentlemen, here is *Sturmmann* Schwenn, he will explain everything and take care of you!" So said *SS-Obersturmführer* Renisch. "First come into the room," I said and led the officers into the spacious cellar room. They were three *Wehrwirtschaftsführer*, all about fifty years old. They had obtained brand-new submachine guns from somewhere and I had to explain to them how they were supposed to be used.

Then we watched about twenty-five Poles who were digging other trenches. A boy of eighteen or nineteen cried without letup. I was then just twenty years old. One of the old men said that he probably thought they would be shot. I replied that all civilians would be evacuated from Warsaw. In some cases, however, the reality was quite different.

Now and then we had heard single shots behind us. We could not associate them with combat, as they were always fired at regular intervals. Then a comrade came to me: "Do you know what's going on? They're killing Poles! Come with me if you don't believe it." So

Above: In the center of the photo is the Senior SS and Police Commander Warthe, *SS-Gruppenführer und Generalleutnant der Waffen-SS und Polizei* Heinz Reinefarth.

Left: *SS-Obergruppenführer und General der Polizei* von dem Bach while commanding general in the Warsaw area.

we went down the stairs of a ruined building and positioned ourselves at the edge of the landing, where the wall to the ruins below had collapsed. They had driven approximately 300 Poles together on a forecourt, and members of the Security Police were shooting them with Beretta submachine guns. Hiwis then began burning the bodies.

In spite of everything, I was shocked. This wasn't something I hadn't seen before, but these civilians were no different than the people who lived with us in Germany. I believe Warsaw was where I woke up. I saw and experienced too many atrocities there. A city was dying and the population was dying day and night.

One time my *Wehrwirtschaftsführer* and I went on patrol around the Belvedere. I heard noises from a manhole cover. No question, it was voices. We listened and lifted up the manhole cover. A dirt-covered face appeared. It looked up, amazed and astonished, and then disappeared again like lightning. Then we took a smoke grenade, walked to another manhole cover and threw it in. Thirty-five to forty Poles came from below ground to the surface, coughing and spluttering. The SD took charge of them.

The fighting in Warsaw was special in another way. Looting was epidemic. It is likely that entire trains loaded with stolen goods went to Germany—valuable paintings, furniture, artwork and luxury articles of every kind. A joke was already circulating which showed how real this was: "What will the planned Warsaw Shield look like? Men leaving a house loaded with booty, and standing on the next corner an officer. Reaching into his mess tin he pulls out Iron Crosses, Second Class and pins them on their tunics."

In the last days of September, all through October, and the first days of November 1944, Warsaw became a witch's cauldron. There was shooting and dying everywhere. Everything that hadn't been blown up was quickly blown up and everywhere fires were started and everything that was combustible was reduced to smoke and ashes.

We received orders to leave Warsaw. Shrouded in smoke and driving through burning streets, we looked for a dump which was supposed to have ammunition. We loaded the boxes into the truck and reached the freight depot where a train was waiting for us. Comrades had already prepared the freight cars—couches and many cartons of cigarettes, crates with wine and liquors of all kinds and luxury articles.

Street fighting in Warsaw 1944.

Evacuation of the Polish population from Warsaw in 1944.

When we departed, we left behind a burning city with desperate survivors. We had waged a war in Warsaw for three full months and several days, without pity and with the result that basically everything had been in vain. We rolled westward through Upper Silesia into Czechoslovakia and the Protectorate of Bohemia and Moravia to SS Training Camp Böhmen.

SS Training Camp Böhmen, 1945

SS Training Camp Böhmen near Beneschau became the SS Cavalry Replacement Battalion's new home in the summer of 1944. The troops were stationed in the towns of Seltschan, Tworschowitz, Jannowitz, Drachkau and Boskowitz. We from the 1942 age class got to know regular barracks and even the recruits of 1944 were relatively well-accommodated in a Warsaw school, but the boys who joined in autumn 1944 and later were denied this. The 2nd (Bicycle-Reconnaissance-Training) Troop was quartered in Drachkau.

Their quarters were abandoned farmer's cottages, from which some of the owners had been forcibly removed. Great emphasis was placed on hygiene, but the lack of facilities made it difficult to realize. To help the men get to sleep, as NSFO (National-Socialist Leadership Officer), *SS-Untersturmführer* Eckhardt, called Poldi, gave boring lectures, quoting from training letters. In the morning Poldi dragged the poor fellows out of their warm stale air for morning exercise. He sent the individual squads on night orientation marches with map and compass. None of the squads got even close to the town Poldi had given as the starting point.

Big regiment-strength exercises were carried out. The battalion had been expanded into the SS Cavalry Training and Replacement Regiment in December 1944. In the process *SS-Sturmbannführer* Plank was promoted to *SS-Obersturmbannführer*. *SS-Obersturmführer* Leifheit had obtained a transfer to the SS Parachute Battalion. Otherwise, all the others were still there, including *SS-Untersturmführer* Glatter. As course inspector, he had led the NCO and Squad Leader Course that had taken place in the 2nd (Bicycle-Reconnaissance-Training) Troop in Warsaw.

Once again we were asked to make young men ready for service at the front. In four to five weeks we were supposed to teach these soldiers, some of whom were just sixteen years old, how a heavy machine gun or medium mortar worked and how to employ them. After I had been at the training camp for about six weeks, as a "Warsaw fighter" I was given fourteen days special leave. I was thus one of the four men who were permitted to go home from December 20, 1944, until January 5, 1945.

The troop subsequently moved to Boskowitz. There we were visited one day by one of the most senior officers of the *Waffen-SS*, *SS-Oberst-Gruppenführer und Generaloberst der Waffen-SS* Paul Hausser.* He was very satisfied with the level of training. We moved again, this time to Tworschowitz Castle. Residing there was the commander of a munitions depot, an *SS-Hauptsturmführer* on the verge of old age. Having successfully completed a non-commissioned officer's course in the summer of 1944, on January 30, 1945, I was promoted to *SS-Unterscharführer*. Thus I was no longer an assistant instructor. Barely twenty-one, I was officially given my own group of recruits to instruct.

We were all placed on alert at the beginning of May 1945. A Czech uprising was expected and this in fact broke out in Prague on May 5. We received mission orders on the seventh. Our primary mission was to escort the German civilians to the west. Outside Prague we put to flight rebels who had occupied a railway station. The trains there included one with German civilians from Silesia. We combed the surrounding houses and found a round, fat fellow who pleaded with us, claiming he had nothing to do with it all. Unfortunately here too we received no orders to act. Then, as we watched the refugee column moving west, he stood behind the stone gateway with a hunting rifle and shot down our popular *SS-Rottenführer* Helmut Enners, before he himself bit the dust.

"You and your squad will be the rear guard!" my troop leader said to me. And then they were gone. I wandered about the area, and at two in the morning I discovered, rather by chance, that the

*Paul Hausser was seriously wounded on August 21, 1944, while serving as Commander-in-Chief of Army Group B in France. While recovering, he visited *Waffen-SS* replacement training units, probably as an inspector. In January 1945, he was appointed commander-in-chief of Army Group Upper Rhine.

war was over. I subsequently assumed that I had completed my assignment and we pedaled back to Tworschowitz Castle.

When we arrived back at our quarters early on May 8, 1945, we found that they had been occupied by Czech nationalists under the command of a colonel. My loudmouth last troop commander, Veit Urban, our first sergeant, and the troop, were gone. So I stood there with my twelve lads, average age seventeen, who had an average of just four weeks training.

And suddenly several cars roared past us. We recognized SS officers, driving west in fully-loaded staff vehicles. They glanced at us from the corners of their eyes and shouted, perhaps to the drivers: "Faster, don't stop!"

Chapter 4
End of the War and Captivity

The Czech colonel, who, thank God, obviously had no feelings of revenge towards us, sent us on our way to the collection camp at Tabor, a former police barracks, with a three-men guard. On the way to Bistrice Market we had stones thrown at us by rabble in the side streets.

Thousands of people were penned together in the collection camp. They were not all soldiers, rather anyone who was in the least German. The Czechs treated the prisoners very badly. It was the Russians who often prevented the worst from happening. The Czechs were also not particularly sympathetic towards them either.

Fortunately I wasn't at Tabor very long. I was packed into a freight train with a mixture of soldiers and civilians, destination unknown. We travelled through Austria, Hungary and later Rumania. Then in Focsani we stood on the square of a barracks camp and received bread and a liter of soup. The wheels rolled again until we arrived at Constanza on the Black Sea. Then about 1,200 members of the defeated German military marched down to the harbor. Behind a warehouse was the Rumanian cruise ship *Transylvania*. We walked up the gangway onto the ship and I took up position at the railing on the promenade deck. At some point the coast of the Crimea appeared. We sailed into port and for a short time were placed in an empty naval school.

That same day we marched around the bay of the port of Sevastopol to a tent camp on a hill. It was summer, it was warm and in fact tolerable. An anti-fascist group was formed and tried to convert us to a new line. Anyone who joined was given three dollops of kasha (buckwheat cereal) instead of one. Despite this their success was limited. Our officers in particular now seemed to realize that communism was the only true path—for three cooking spoons of kasha.

We put up roof structures and built cisterns. By and by we were taken to the prison in Sevastopol for interrogation. A few words about our treatment by the Russians. Our guards and the civilians we met were not as brutal as our former allies the Hungarians, some of whom were employed as functionaries. The Russians often had it little better than us. Soon after the surrender it turned out that our *Ostmärker* (residents of Austria after the *Anschluss*), who in 1938, could scarcely have screamed "Heil Hitler" any louder, had suddenly become "Austrians" and wanted nothing more to do with us Germans. The Russians, who at least usually respected an honorable opinion, then placed the Austrians in the same category as the Rumanians, which meant that they received less food than we Germans … the "Austrians" had cut off their noses to spite their faces.

After I had slaved away in the shipyard (here too the Russian sailors often slipped us something, I was moved to the camp in the middle of Sevastopol. It was surrounded by some more or less collapsed houses, but the food was well-cooked and the bread was better than in the first camp.

In 1946, word suddenly came that we were going home. Before our camp's gate stood sixty men—I and a comrade from the 8th SS Cavalry Division "Florian Geyer" among them. Unfortunately, only fifty-eight marched out through the gate. Gerhard and I remained and were interrogated briefly. They had probably remembered that we had belonged to the *Waffen-SS*.

We were loaded into a truck and taken to the inner courtyard of the Sevastopol prison. Soon afterwards I was in a cell on the second floor. There was a tiny window and a dim light, two sacks filled with sawdust and a bucket for nature's call. I was first joined in my cell by an ethnic German from the Crimea, then a very unpleasant Hungarian with a criminal's face and finally a nice Rumanian.

I was interrogated about my time as a member of the 5th Troop of the 1st SS Cavalry Regiment during the actions in the Pripyat Marshes. I sat before a young lieutenant of the MVD (formerly the NKVD) and a female interpreter. He proved to be surprisingly well informed. He named all the villages in which I had been. Contrary to what any defense attorney would have advised me, when I was asked if I had been present for the burning of villages, the requisitioning of cattle and the shooting of civilians I answered "yes."

The court hearing followed on June 2, 1948. While the average soldier received the blanket sentence of twenty-five years in a labor camp, I and five other members of the 8th SS Cavalry Division were given our own trial. Behind a table covered with a red cloth sat a major and two captains. On the right was the defense counsel and on the left the interpreter. The crimes with which we were charged, which had obviously been committed by members of the 1st SS Cavalry Regiment, were read out to us.* These included charges which, in my opinion, were pure communist propaganda. There was no denying that civilians (partisan sympathizers) had been executed, but by no stretch of the imagination could I imagine that a Russian woman's breasts had been cut off. We were members of this regiment and were therefore sentenced with it, even though it

*A military tribunal of the MVD units of the Polessk Oblast charged the 1st SS Cavalry Regiment with the following crimes against humanity and war crimes:

In May to June 1943, 145 civilians were shot or burned alive in the Lelcickiy District of the Polessk Oblast, twelve villages were burned down including Zabrode, Zalonon, Stodolici, Usov, Ol'chovaya, Zmurnoe, Berestyanskiy zavod and others.

In addition, in the village of Stodolici forty-seven women, children, and old people were shot by soldiers of the regiment, six elderly persons were found buried alive in the ground. Four young girls were raped by an (entire) group; a bestial crime was committed against captured partisan Saraj. His hands and feet were tied to horses and he was torn to pieces. In the village of Loknica they tortured and killed twenty-two men; in the village of Berestyanskiy zavod a bloody deed was carried out against citizen Akulic, Josef. The Germans pulled off his arms, poked out his eyes and struck him on the skull with a rifle butt; in the same village soldiers of the division raped a young woman, cut off her breasts, and then shot her.

It is impossible to determine if all of these crimes were in fact committed and if so whether they involved members of the 1st SS Cavalry Regiment. But as German documents concerning the results of "Operations Vistula I and II" record 1,256 dead partisans and 206 captured against just twenty-two German dead and fifty-six wounded, unfortunately there is a not entirely unfounded basis for such charges.

was never proved that we had played an active part. I imagine that every member of the regiment captured by the Russians received the same sentence. Perhaps in my case the sentence was due to my statement in my first interrogation in 1946, that I had witnessed the burning down of villages, the requisitioning of cattle and the shooting of civilians.

They rose and then came the sentence. I was found guilty on all counts and sentenced to death by firing squad. I was shocked! However, as there was a new decree by the Supreme Soviet, the sentence was reduced to twenty-five years imprisonment in a labor and improvement camp. That put an end to thoughts of quickly going home like other prisoners of war.

We were subsequently transported to Simferopol. We six convicted were sent together to a camp outside the city. Our barrack held 120 men and we felt completely lost. This was only a transit camp, however, and we were sent on to Kharkov. We kneeled on the asphalt of the platform and travelers bustled around us. They scarcely noticed us, as we were kneeling, our shaven heads sunk in a dirty coat and lice-infested shirt and pants.

We arrived in the inner courtyard of a prison and received verbal abuse from the windows. As all the cells were overcrowded, we were placed in the cellar. There we took a bath. As we prisoners could not always step out when we wanted, other prisoners were not the only ones who had gone in their pants. I was given new clothes and then shared a cell with about twenty Russian criminals. Surprisingly they left me in peace and soon after we were sent via Vologda to Vorkuta.

Beginning in August 1949, there I was to serve my twenty-five years according to the will of Stalin. Vorkuta was about seventy-five miles north of the Arctic Circle. We were initially taken to an isolation room for disinfection. After that we were let into the camp, which was attached to a brick works. I was assigned to Barrack 13. The very next day we began working at a conveyor. About 200 yards long, it took away excavated material from a clay quarry.

The clay was loaded into tipper trucks, which had to cover a distance of about 1.25 miles over a cable railway. Then sawdust was mixed in, and the bricks were pressed into form. Piled on wooden slats, the bricks were placed in the drying chamber and then in the circular kiln for firing. Unfortunately the process was easily bungled, and if it rained or snowed the incompletely-baked bricks stuck together and turned into big lumps.

The Vorkuta camp, which previously had housed mainly Russian criminals, increasingly became a German prisoner of war camp. In typical German fashion the prisoners began beautifying the quarters, making them livable. I met *Generaloberst* Jänicke. He was the barrack senior and worked as a guard in the drying chamber. He knit sweaters and taught me how to knit.

I also ran into *SS-Unterscharführer* Masse again. I had first met him as an *SS-Rottenführer* in March 1943. He really was an unpleasant person, who was not only a primitive blackguard but a sadist as well. In the Vorkuta camp he was also known as a notorious liar and thief.

Then I was a member of Erich Leonhardt's Udarnik Brigade. He had been sent to the concentration camps as a career criminal. A notorious capo, he and his former officers were sentenced to life imprisonment. Leonhardt was not physically abusive, in fact he was even friendly and comradely with his men. But to me he was a criminal. I was sitting in our barrack, when a former *Wehrmacht* major appeared. "Quick, quick, get up. Erich is waiting, we must go to work. Get moving, Erich is already impatient." I couldn't believe what I was hearing. "Erich, Erich is waiting?" Had the major lost all five senses? A major was the messenger for a career criminal among us?

While we were fed regularly, there was not an excess gram of fat on us shaven *Woina Plennis* (Russian for prisoners of war). I was repeatedly sent to the infirmary on account of dystrophy. One day I broke a lower leg and was sent to the tailor shop, where I mended the clothes of my fellow prisoners. My time in Vorkuta ended in August 1950, and a train carrying prisoners took me to Stalingrad.

On September 9, 1950, the doors of the freight car were pushed open and then we walked through the streets in high summer temperatures, our heads shaven and wearing quilted jackets and felt boots. When we crossed paths with a group of so-called old Stalingrad prisoners, our appearance amused them terribly. We finally arrived at our new camp above the gorge, at the edge of the inner city. It was squalid, like all the camps in the USSR. We were counted and after it was verified that we were all present we were allowed to bathe. An hour after we had been allocated barracks, we stood in line for assignment to the brigades.

The female camp doctor wrote me into Category III: fit for light work only. I was assigned to a painting brigade, where I mixed paint and cleaned brushes. During our clearing work we, of course, had plenty of contact with the civilian population and despite the fact that the Germans had leveled Stalingrad, they were decent to us. The camp command was also decent. We were finally able to wash our hair again. What a luxury! There was a library and now and then a film was shown in the dining hall. And … we received packages from Germany. They were filled with all the things that were again available at home: *Schoka-Bona* (similar to modern-day "Nutella"), pumpernickel, ham with egg in a can, butter and cream cheese, milk chocolate. Since 1945, the Soviet population had now and then slipped us something, and now we were able to return the favor, pressing this or that into the hands of children and women.

Cultural activities were held and we played soccer. We were able to write home, receive packages and even earned our own money. The maximum allowable sum was 198 rubles, which we received in the first ten days of each month. We could use it to buy candy, bread and margarine and even canned sausages now and then. There was no gluttony to be sure, but one had something extra and could make one's own decisions.

One day a comrade whispered to me that our former regimental commander, Papa Lombard,* was in the camp. Still a good cavalryman,

* Gustav Lombard (April 10, 1895 – September 18, 1992) for a time lived unrecognized in the Soviet prisoner of war camp in Akamara under the assumed name *Major* Müller. His former aide-de-camp *SS-Sturmbannführer* Wolf was transferred to Akamara in 1947, and reported him to the Soviet authorities. In 1947, Lombard was sentenced to twenty-five years imprisonment for the rape and murder of a Russian woman and the shooting of civilians by members of the 1st SS Cavalry Regiment. On October 10, 1955, he was finally released from the Voykovo prisoner of war camp as part of the amnesty for German prisoners negotiated by Adenauer. In 1962, the Munich I public prosecutor's office began looking into his actions in the Pripyat region. The trial was halted on December 22, 1970, as "a particularly barbaric crime or base motive," could not be proved, therefore he could not be charged with murder. The statute of limitations made it impossible to charge him for any other possible crimes.

I went to see him. He had set himself up in the rearmost room with the other generals. I found a sick old man sitting on the bed. He no longer understood the world and dismissed one and all. When he was apprehended by the politruks he is supposed to have said, "A German pig betrayed me." My old platoon leader Zeno Alberti told me this.

So a "German pig," as our commander liked to put it, had betrayed him to the Russians. What had our *Papachen* (little father) expected? While the simple cavalrymen were sentenced to death for the orders he had given us and then were held as slaves in the worker's and farmer's paradise of the USSR until 1956, he lived better, did not have to work, received general's rations, slept in a warm room and cared not a whit about his former subordinates.

I visited him in his quarters and afterward turned away with horror. He sat among the other "innocents" and cursed every one of his former subordinates, for they had "done it." He hadn't shot the civilians, burned down the villages and requisitioned the cattle! Therefore we simple marchers should take the blame alone!

Our camp was disbanded in autumn 1953. About half of the prisoners were finally allowed to go home and we went to the camp opposite the tractor works on the bank of the Volga. The generals, staff officers and men of the former 6th Army, or at least those who had survived, lived there in tidy earth barracks and stone structures. At the end of the year a staff officer who had returned home wrote to his comrades back in Stalingrad Camp 1: " … and I very much miss our interesting discussions in the evening!" As absurd as that sounds, after my return home in 1956 I also felt a sense of loneliness, no longer sitting with comrades at many discussions, conversations with people with whom I and many of my comrades would otherwise never have spent time with in our lives.

I was assigned to a clean earth barrack and was given the upper bunk above the lecturer Doctor of Philosophy Schmitz, whose education then also expanded mine. The receipt of packages was now not unusual. Packages came from the Red Cross, from the Workers' Welfare Association, from the Catholic Church and from family. Only I received none. All I received from my parents were cards with blah-blah, which said nothing. In hope of also being able to enjoy such cards, I found an address in Hamburg and sent a card to an alleged relative. It paid off, for this made them aware of the fact that I was a poor prisoner of war whose relatives had probably been killed in Hamburg … I finally received a package, which halfway through the month was a nice supplement to my rations. The package inspections were undertaken very liberally.

In January 1954, we were moved to the Urals. During the trip in freight cars, to the left and right I saw only snow and the familiar Soviet expanses and endlessness. Everything looked to us uninhabited and bleak. Where are you God? You the almighty? Rumors circulated that we were going home too. We hoped until the last moment: were we going home? The train halted again. It shunted, forward and back. Then the train stopped. The doors were thrown open: *"Davai, davai!"* ("Come on, come on"). We stood at a construction materials depot, formed ourselves into the familiar rows of five and walked along the tracks. Thirty minutes later we came to a camp gate.

We were assigned to centrally-heated rooms, ten to each one. We had stayed in worse. The usual procedure began. We were registered and asked for our personal information. It was cold and snowing. Our guards had their fur collars turned up and we were wearing our padded jackets and caps. Once again we never heard an angry word from the guards or the population. Once, when a drunk called us "fascists," our column leader pushed him into our midst and called: "Go ahead, give him a couple in the mouth!" We didn't, instead we shoved the vodka lover back out of the column. We emptied rail cars carrying clinkers and sand, lifted beams from trucks and for weeks hammered frozen gravel from flatcars.

After I received nothing from my parents apart from trivial postcards, and as I also had no interest in settling in the newly-created German Democratic Republic, I sent all of my postcards to my friend Rudi Molle, who I had met as a prisoner of war but who had been released, in Wuppertal. Once again I played a trick and wrote the following address on the postcards: *Herr* Wilhelm Schwenn, Wuppertal-Elberfeld, Hospitalstrasse 9 c/o Molle.

I could then say that my relatives lived in West Germany. On March 26, 1955, I became thirty-one years old—I had been a prisoner of war of the Soviets for almost ten years. Two friends came with a half liter of vodka (Moskava brand)—what a surprise—what joy. For a few hours we forgot the whole shitty situation we were in.

And once again there came another camp. But this time I had the feeling that it would be the last one! Germany won the world soccer championship in the summer of 1954. Our standing with the Russians rose sharply. We received more and more privileges, we even had radios in our rooms, watches on our wrists and in our vest pockets. Gloves, stylish leather shoes and scarves were not uncommon among us prisoners.

My motivation was nearing the zero mark, however. I could not understand why all of my superiors, even the generals and staff officers, were sent home before the last of us *Woinna Plennies*. And so I repeatedly refused to work, which was punished by detention. This did, however, give me a break from the tootling of the radios in the barracks and the chatter of my comrades. By then they were already getting on my nerves too. I stuck with my more educated comrades and spoke about esthetic things.

A friend said to me: "There's someone in the main hospital who wants to see you!" I went there and saw my old platoon leader Zeno Alberti. He was lying in bed and grinned happily when he saw me. Zeno talked with his hands and feet like an Italian: "Papa Lombard got his 25 years too!" "I know Zeno, I saw him in the Stalingrad camp. He wasn't the same Papa though." Had our comrade *SS-Standartenführer* Lombard believed that he would get off unscathed? You stood at attention for years, carried out the orders which people like Lombard issued. Then the war was lost, and everything you had done was suddenly bad. Your own former superiors stood up and declared: "It wasn't me, it was the *Rottenführer*, the *Sturmmann*, the cavalryman, the *Unterscharführer*, it was them."

One evening after returning from our place of work, we were summoned to the administration building. We were sent alphabetically to different rooms. In mine sat a political officer and beside him a comrade from the clothing store, who spoke perfect Russian. He asked me: "To where do you want to be released? Probably somewhere in the west?" "Well, I would like … " "Hold your tongue. In the west then. Where?" "Wuppertal." Good, now take off, don't keep me here!" A delicate seedling of hope bestirred itself. The political officer had not shown the slightest interest in the questioning. He had sat there, playing with a pencil, looking bored and staring out the window.

Then came Adenauer's visit to the USSR. He wanted to bring the last 10,000 prisoners of war home. He and his delegation arrived in Moscow on September 9, 1955. The next day when he asked that the last prisoners of war be released, Bulganin said that there were no more prisoners of war in the USSR, only war criminals whose crimes were so terrible that one dreaded even talking about the subject. Our chancellor did the only correct thing and announced that he was returning home. The Soviets back-pedaled, for they were probably hoping for economic aid from the west. "That's not what was meant," said Khrushchev.

A transport to the DDR (German Democratic Republic) was first assembled and dispatched, however most of the men—including me—wanted to go to the west. A second followed, this time to the BRD (Federal Republic of Germany). Others followed to the west, and finally there were only 300 to 400 of us left. Suddenly, it was said that the transports had been stopped because Adenauer had not lived up to his obligations. And I was now among the last of the last … I was probably classified as an especially evil subject.

The days and weeks passed, our nerves dragged on the ground. I scarcely left the barracks and by then we didn't work any more. Packages also stopped coming, as the last prisoners of war had supposedly long since returned home. It snowed and fat flakes fell from the sky. Christmas 1955 passed without notice, the year 1956 began. In two months and twenty-six days, I would be able to celebrate my thirty-third birthday. I had become a soldier at the age of nineteen.

Then on January 5, 1956, something happened. We heard our names called out and each was given a card. On mine was "Car 6, Seat 26." And so I was worthy to go home. I had slowly arrived at the conclusion that I was the most evil of all war criminals. The snow lay deep in the camp, high snowbanks lined the camp streets, and on them lay our sawdust-filled mattresses and beside them our wooden suitcases. Everything lay there in the morning, the afternoon and the evening. The loading detachments returned from the rail station: "No, still no cars there and no locomotive!" There was panic, mistrust and fear: "Oh dear God, let it come true, our return home after so many years!" In the stove in our quarters there was a crackling fire, from time to time a piece of wood was added. Some men sat at the table, others lay on the bare bed frames. Then there was movement in the gloom outside. I opened the door and suddenly heard: "Who is for Car 6? To the gate immediately!" "What, Car 6?" That was mine. I collected my bag with hand towel and washing things and sprinted to the gate. The person on guard checked off our names from a list and we climbed into a truck and were driven to a track at the freight yard. Sitting there was the transport train—to our great surprise there were passenger cars and not freight cars. Via Sverdlovsk, Kazan, Gorki, Moscow, Smolensk, Orsha and Minsk we arrived at the Soviet–Polish border near Brest.

The hydraulic brakes hissed, the locomotive and cars slowed, and the train came to a stop. There the railroad tracks changed from the Soviet gauge to normal West-European gauge. I picked up my luggage and with my comrades walked over the platform. As we weren't allowed to take rubles out of the country, we went into a sales pavilion and bought sweets, fish and cheese. An hour passed and then we rolled slowly out of the station. We crossed the Bug at a walking pace. With several short stops at various stations we approached the former German border. The fields lay fallow, the towns wasted. Everywhere there was dirt and grime, untended gardens. Then we reached the new German-Polish border at Frankfurt/Oder.

Slowly, almost carefully, our transport train rolled into the freight yard. In a gloomy warehouse we got a new locomotive and after an hour we carried on. Finally, on January 16, 1956, we arrived at Herleshausen Station. Countless people were waiting for us, laughing and crying, "Welcome, welcome!" Many held up desperate signs: "Who knows my son, my husband, my father … ? You are the last, you must know him!" A class of schoolgirls stood there and sang folksongs. My eyes became damp. With a mug of tea with rum in one hand and a roll with a giant sausage in the other, I climbed into one of the buses which took us to the Friedland camp.

Leading the way were three motorcycle-sidecars of the ADAC, police cars, and finally we in the buses. The towns through which we drove were decorated, garlands and banners hung everywhere. Federal border guards lined the road, church bells rang. Oh my God, that I have lived to see this! I had dreamed of it for years. The bus stopped on a large square in the Friedland camp. We climbed out and sang: “Now Thank We All Our God” and the third stanza of the German national anthem. Then the receptions began. There were people waiting for us … either friends, family or the police, who immediately arrested particularly notorious criminals like Gustav Sorge and Kurt Ekarius. They were later tried by West German courts. There was no one waiting for me, or was there? My parents were in East Germany and I had almost no close contacts in West Germany. And yet there was someone waiting for me. Erhard, my friend of many years through captivity, had arrived in Friedland two days before me and now gave me a warm welcome.

I sent two telegrams, one to my parents in Seebad Ahlbeck and one to my friend Rudi Molle in Wuppertal. My parents were surely disappointed that I stayed in the west, but even though I longed to again hear the crash of waves on the Baltic shore, I had little desire for the notoriety I would gain there: “Look, that’s Willi Schwenn’s boy. He was held prisoner by the Russians. Yes, yes, he was supposed to be a war criminal!”

Rudi Molle called me at the camp: “Come here to Wuppertal immediately!” I thanked him but said no. They were looking after me here and I didn’t have to worry about anything. Then I took a train to nearby Göttingen. After almost eleven years I wanted to be a free man again and be able to move about on my own. Finally we were transferred out of the Friedland camp. I went to Westernkotten and was housed with eleven other late returnees in the spa house. We were sitting having lunch when I was called to the telephone. It was my mother: “We’re here!” “Where?” “At the station in Lippstadt.” In fact they had received a travel permit, probably to bring their son back to the beautiful DDR. Now they sat and looked expectantly at their son: “Say something son, do something. We want to begin a new life with you.” No, there was nothing doing. I am not the one who has to look after you. You had eleven years time to go to the west, and “when the boy comes home, he shall find a home in freedom.” No, they had made a home in a converted stable. “No mother and father, I’m sorry. I have enough problems of my own.” There was nothing to do. I sent them home again. We spent several pleasant days together, then they left. The day after, my conscience bothered me. But then I said to myself: “It’s not your fault. Sit there and say nothing, don’t be sad. One would like to help, but one has misgivings. So do nothing.”

My stay there ended and finally I was on a train to Wuppertal. It stopped in Elberfeld and my friend Rudi was standing there waiting for me. We clapped each other hard on the shoulders. There were candles burning in the entire house, on the door was "Welcome!" and I could scarcely close my mouth, in which about fifteen teeth had broken off during my captivity. Soon afterwards a dentist pulled them and before too long I had my third set of teeth in my mouth.

At the employment office they offered me a caretaker position, which I gladly accepted. At the housing office I was given a small room at Wiesenstrasse 101 in Wuppertal-Elberfeld. I bought an NSU Quick moped and was happy and satisfied with myself and the world. I applied for admission to the customs training school in Bad Gandersheim and in November 1957, I received my certificate of appointment to customs candidate and civil service candidate from the head of the school, Regierungsrat Kulitscher. In the middle grade of the service I rose to customs chief secretary. In 1985, I was

*On October 18, 1991, the Russian Federation passed a law "Concerning the Rehabilitation of Victims of Political Repression." Initially limited to its own citizens, in December 1992, the law's scope was extended to include foreign citizens. This included the approximately 2.5 million German prisoners of war. Decisions concerning the rehabilitation of foreigners were made on a strictly individual basis, based on the concrete materials in the archived criminal files and whether there was proof of guilt. According to Colonel of Justice Leonid P. Kopalin, head of the Foreign Rehabilitation Department, 13,000 applications were processed by the end of 1998. Of these applicants, 8,820 were rehabilitated, and 2,530 were denied rehabilitation. Applications from foreigners fell under the following categories:

1. Crimes against the state (counterrevolutionary crimes), as envisaged in the RSFSR criminal code of 1926, in particular armed uprising or entry into Soviet territory, espionage, terror attacks, anti-Soviet propaganda, sabotage, etc.

2. Crimes associated with acts of cruelty against the population and captured members of the Red Army, as described in the decree by the Presidium of the Supreme Soviet of April 19, 1943: "Concerning measures to punish German fascist criminals, who are guilty of having committed acts of murder and ill-treatment against the Soviet civilian population and against captured members of the Red Army, to punish spies and traitors to the Fatherland from the ranks of Soviet citizens and their accomplices."

interviewed by NDR reporter Hannelore Schäfer and interview was broadcast under the title "My Own History." In forty-five minutes I described my almost eleven years as a prisoner of war.

At the beginning of the 1990s, one could apply to the Russian Federation for rehabilitation from sentences imposed by the USSR.* I made an application by way of the German embassy in Moscow. Had I expected anything else but rejection?

Translation Decision No.
The Military Court Attached to Unit 16666

Has at its session on October 13, 1995, under Colonel of Justice S.D. Litvinov, in the presence of the two Colonels of Justice A.A. Sboew and L.G. Yevdokimov and the chief consultant of the military state prosecutor with Unit 52740, Colonel of Justice M.M. Sisow, reviewed

3. War and other crimes as per Control Council Act No. December 10–20, 1945: "Concerning the punishment of persons, who are guilty of having committed war crimes, crimes against peace and against humanity."

4. General Criminal Crimes (property crimes, crimes against the person etc.). Citizens who were justifiably punished as per the criminal code for the named offenses will not be rehabilitated. As per Article 4 of the rehabilitation law, such persons who were justifiably sentenced by courts can not be rehabilitated if there is in their file sufficient proof for a charge of using force against the civilian population or prisoners of war, war crimes, crimes against peace and humanity. Such files are checked particularly carefully, for when an application for rehabilitation is submitted it can only be denied by a court based on the expertise of a state prosecutor. As is well known, military members of enemy armies fighting against the USSR committed many atrocities, which in keeping with international law and criminal legislation of the Russian Federation are justifiably classified by as most serious crimes. Such persons were found among the prisoners of war and internees and have received their just sentences. The overwhelming majority of the non-rehabilitated Germans and Austrians are former members of the German Army, who are guilty of having committed war crimes and crimes against humanity.

Embassy of the
Federal Republic
of Germany

Moscow
November 24, 1995

To Herr Albert Schwenn

Subject: Rehabilitation of Germans sentenced by Soviet military tribunals or pursued by the NKVD;

Here: Herr Albert Schwenn

Concerning: Our letter of June 23, 1995

Dear Herr Schwenn,

We have received a copy of the ruling by the responsible military court of the Russian Federation, which states that rehabilitation for Herr Albert Schwenn has been denied. We regret this decision and please take note that we have included a copy of the ruling and an unauthorized translation.

Yours sincerely,

2

Рассмотрев материалы дела, обсудив ходатайство посольства ФРГ и заключение прокурора, военный суд - войсковая часть 16666 находит приговор в отношении ШВЕНА законным и обоснованным.

Вина ШВЕНА в совершении преступления, за которое он осужден, подтверждена собранными по делу доказательствами, достоверность которых сомнений не вызывает.

Так, будучи неоднократно допрошенным в ходе предварительного следствия ШВЕН показывал, что проходя службу в войсках СС во время войны Германии с СССР он со своими сослуживцами лично принимал участие в расстрелах мирных советских граждан на временно оккупированной территории СССР.

В частности ШВЕН показывал, что в 1943 году участвовал в расстреле 200 граждан возле деревни Лапичи, угоне их скота и разграблении имущества, а также летом 1943 года участвовал в расстреле 40 граждан возле деревни Штудоличи, которая была разграблена и сожжена.

При этом ШВЕН давал достаточно подробные показания о местах, времени и обстоятельствах этих действий и пояснял, что он принимал в этом непосредственное участие в качестве пулеметчика карательной команды (л.д.93, 98-99, 103, 107-108).

Эти свои показания ШВЕН подтвердил и в судебном заседании, хотя и пояснил, что не проявлял активности (л,д.316-317).

О расстреле из пулеметов 200 мирных советских граждан эсэсовцами в 1943 году возле деревни Лапичи показали свидетели - жители соседних белорусских деревень СТЕШКО, ШАМАК, ГОМОК.

Как видно из сообщения Лапичского сельсовета Осиповического района Белорусской ССР от 18 декабря 1946 года в 1943 году немецким карательным отрядом возле реки Свисючи было расстреляно 200 советских граждан, сожжена деревня и угнан скот.

При таких обстоятельствах следует признать, что ШВЕН осужден за содеянное обоснованно, его преступным действиям дана правильная юридическая оценка и назначено справедливое наказание.

Поэтому ШВЕН не является жертвой политических репрессий и реабилитации не подлежит.

На основании изложенного и руководствуясь ст.ст.377,378 УПК РФ, ст.4,п."б", [illegible],п."а", 10 Закона РСФСР от 18 октября 1991 года "О реабилитации жертв политических репрессий", военный суд - войсковая часть 16666

О П Р Е Д Е Л И Л :

Признать ШВЕН Альберта обоснованно осужденным по настоящему делу и не подлежащим реабилитации.

Определение может быть опротестовано прокурором и обжаловано заинтересованными лицами и общественными организациями в Военную коллегию Верховного Суда Российской Федерации.

Подлинное за надлежащими подписями.

С подлинным верно: ЧЛЕН ВОЕННОГО СУДА - ВОЙСКОВАЯ ЧАСТЬ 16666
полковник юстиции
Л.ЕВДОКИМОВ

2

Рассмотрев материалы дела, обсудив ходатайство посольства ФРГ и заключение прокурора, военный суд - войсковая часть 16666 находит приговор в отношении ШВЕНА законным и обоснованным.

Вина ШВЕНА в совершении преступления, за которое он осужден, подтверждена собранными по делу доказательствами, достоверность которых сомнений не вызывает.

Так, будучи неоднократно допрошенным в ходе предварительного следствия ШВЕН показывал, что проходя службу в войсках СС во время войны Германии с СССР он со своими сослуживцами лично принимал участие в расстрелах мирных советских граждан на временно оккупированной территории СССР.

В частности ШВЕН показывал, что в 1943 году участвовал в расстреле 200 граждан возле деревни Лапичи, угоне их скота и разграблении имущества, а также летом 1943 года участвовал в расстреле 40 граждан возле деревни Штудоличи, которая была разграблена и сожжена.

При этом ШВЕН давал достаточно подробные показания о местах, времени и обстоятельствах этих действий и пояснял, что он принимал в этом непосредственное участие в качестве пулеметчика карательной команды (л.д.93, 98-99, 103, 107-108).

Эти свои показания ШВЕН подтвердил и в судебном заседании, хотя и пояснил, что не проявлял активности (л,д.316-317).

О расстреле из пулеметов 200 мирных советских граждан эсэсовцами в 1943 году возле деревни Лапичи показали свидетели - жители соседних белорусских деревень СТЕШКО, ШАМАК, ГОМОК.

Как видно из сообщения Лапичского сельсовета Осиповического района Белорусской ССР от 18 декабря 1946 года в 1943 году немецким карательным отрядом возле реки Свисючи было расстреляно 200 советских граждан, сожжена деревня и угнан скот.

При таких обстоятельствах следует признать, что ШВЕН осужден за содеянное обоснованно, его преступным действиям дана правильная юридическая оценка и назначено справедливое наказание.

Поэтому ШВЕН не является жертвой политических репрессий и реабилитации не подлежит.

На основании изложенного и руководствуясь ст.ст.377,378 УПК РФ, ст.4,п."б", 8,п."а", 10 Закона РСФСР от 18 октября 1991 года "О реабилитации жертв политических репрессий", военный суд - войсковая часть 16666

ОПРЕДЕЛИЛ:

Признать ШВЕН Альберта обоснованно осужденным по настоящему делу и не подлежащим реабилитации.

Определение может быть опротестовано прокурором и обжаловано заинтересованными лицами и общественными организациями в Военную коллегию Верховного Суда Российской Федерации.

Подлинное за надлежащими подписями.

С подлинным верно: ЧЛЕН ВОЕННОГО СУДА - ВОЙСКОВАЯ ЧАСТЬ 16666
полковник юстиции
Л.ЕВДОКИМОВ

Übersetzung

Entscheidung Nr.
Das Militärgericht beim Truppenteil Nr. 16666

hat unter Vorsitz des Oberst der Justiz S.D. Litwinow, im Beisein der beiden Obersten der Justiz A.A. Sboew und L.G. Jewdokimow sowie des Hauptreferenten des Militärstaatsanwalts beim Truppenteil 52740, Oberst der Justiz M.M. Sisow, in seiner Sitzung am 13.10.1995 den Rehabilitationsantrag der Deutschen Botschaft und den Beschluß des Stellvertretenden Hauptmilitärstaatsanwalts in der Strafsache gegen den dt. Staatsangehörigen Albert SCHWEN, geb. 1924 in Swinemünde, Deutschland, damaliger Kriegsgefangener,
der am 02.06.1948 vom Militärgericht der Truppen des Innenministeriums der Krim gemäß § 1 des Erlasses des Präsidiums des Obersten Sowjets der UdSSR vom 19.04.1943 zu einer Haftstrafe von 25 Jahren in einem Arbeits- und Besserungslager verurteilt worden war, behandelt.

Das Urteil wurde nicht angefochten.

Nach den Ausführungen des Oberst der Justiz JEWDOKIMOW und des Staatsanwalts zur Begründung des Widerspruchs hat das Militärgericht beim Truppenteil 16666

festgestellt:

Gemäß Gerichtsurteil ist SCHWEN schuldig befunden worden, da er, im Militärdienst der deutschen Armee in der 8. Kavalleriedivision der SS "Florian Geyer" in der 5. Schwadron des 8. Kavallerieregiments im Rang eines Rottenführers stehend, 1943 aktiv an der Massenvernichtung friedlicher Bürger, der Verschleppung sowjetischer Bürger nach Deutschland und der Zerstörung von Dörfern teilgenommen hat.
So hat Schwen im April 1943 als Angehöriger einer Sonderstrafeinheit in der Weißrussischen SSR im Bezirk Ossipowitsch an der Erschießung von 200 Sowjetbürgern und der Plünderung ihres Eigentums teilgenommen.
Im Juni 1943 war er an der Erschießung von 40 Sowjetbürgern in der Nähe des Dorfes Schtudolitschi im Bezirk Petrikowo der Weißrussischen SSR beteiligt.
Die Deutsche Botschaft beantragt die Rehabilitierung von SCHWEN.
Der stellv. Hauptmilitärstaatsanwalt bittet in seinem Schlußwort, das Urteil des Militärgerichts gegen SCHWEN nicht zu ändern und ihn nicht zu rehabilitieren.

Das Militärgericht beim Truppenteil 16666 hält nach Erörterung des Antrags der Deutschen Botschaft und des Schlußworts des stellv. Hauptmilitärstaatsanwalts und nach Prüfung der Unterlagen das Urteil gegen SCHWEN für gerechtfertigt und begründet.

Die Schuld SCHWENs an den begangenen Verbrechen, für die er verurteilt wurde, wird durch die in dieser Sache zusammengetragenen Beweise gestützt, an deren Echtheit kein Zweifel besteht.
So hat Schwen mehrfach während der Verhöre im Laufe der Untersuchungen angegeben, mit seinen Kameraden während des Krieges gegen die UdSSR als SS-Angehöriger an der Erschießung friedlicher Sowjetbürger auf dem zeitweilig besetzten Gebiet der UdSSR teilgenommen zu haben.
SCHWEN hat insbesondere angegeben, 1943 an der Erschießung von 200 Menschen beim Dorf Lapitschi, bei der Eintreibung ihres Viehs und der Plünderung ihres Besitzes

teilgenommen zu haben. Ebenso sei er im Sommer 1943 an der Erschießung von 40 Menschen beim Dorf Schtudolitschi, das geplündert und verbrannt wurde, beteiligt gewesen. Dabei machte SCHWEN genaueste Angaben über Orte, den Zeitpunkt und die Umstände dieser Verbrechen und gab zu, als MG-Schütze des Strafkommandos persönlich beteiligt gewesen zu sein.
Diese Angaben machte SCHWEN auch während der Gerichtsverhandlung, gab aber an, nicht aktiv gewesen zu sein. Bewohner von weißrussischen Nachbardörfern sagten bei der Verhandlung als Zeugen aus und bestätigten die Erschießung von 200 Personen.

Unter diesen Umständen muß gefolgert werden, daß SCHWEN begründertermaßen verurteilt und daß sein verbrecherisches Handeln juristisch korrekt bewertet wurde.
SCHWEN ist kein Opfer politischer Repression und unterliegt somit nicht der Rehabilitierung.

Gemäß dem Ausgeführten sowie §§ 377 und 378 der Strafprozeßordnung der RF, § 4b, § 9a und § 10 des Gesetzes der RSFSR vom 18.10.1991 "Über die Rehabilitierung von Opfern politischer Repressionen" hat das Militärgericht beim Truppenteil 16666

e n t s c h i e d e n:

Albert SCHWEN wurde in der vorliegenden Strafsache begründetermaßen verurteilt und unterliegt nicht der Rehabilitierung.

Gegen den Beschluß können betroffene Personen oder gesellschaftliche Organisationen beim Militärkollegium des Obersten Gerichts der Russischen Föderation Widerspruch einlegen.

Original mit entsprechenden Unterschriften.

Übereinstimmung mit dem Original: (Siegel)
Mitglied. des Militärgerichts beim Truppenteil 16666

(Unterschrift) L. Jewdokimow
Oberst der Justiz

the application from the German embassy and the decision of the acting military state prosecutor in the criminal case against the German citizen Albert SCHWENN, born in Swinemünde in 1924, former prisoner of war,

Who on June 2, 1948, was sentenced to 25 years in a labor and improvement camp by the military court of the troops of the Ministry of the Interior in Crimea as per § 1 of the decree of the Presidium of the Supreme Soviet of the USSR of April 19, 1943.

The sentence was not appealed.

According to Colonel of Justice YEVDOKIMOV and the state prosecutor, in support of its opposition the military court attached to Unit 16666 found that:

As per the sentence of the court, SCHWENN was found guilty as he, in the military service of the German Army in the 8th SS Cavalry Division "Florian Geyer" with the rank of *Rottenführer*, in 1943, actively participated in the mass murder of peaceful citizens, the removal of Soviet citizens to Germany and the destruction of villages.

In April 1943, as a member of a punishment unit in the district of Osipovich in the White Russian Soviet Socialist Republic, Schwenn took part in the shooting of 200 Soviet citizens and the plundering of their property.

In June 1943, he participated in the shooting of forty Soviet citizens near the village of Shtudolichi in the Petrikovo District of White Russia.

The German embassy requests the rehabilitation of SCHWENN.

In his conclusion, the deputy military state prosecutor requested that the military court's sentence against SCHWENN not be changed and that he not be rehabilitated.

After considering the German embassy's application and the deputy military state prosecutor's closing statement and reviewing the documents, the military court attached to Unit 16666 finds the sentence against SCHWENN to be justified and reasonable.

SCHWENN's guilt in the crimes of which he was sentenced is supported by the proof assembled for this case, in whose veracity there is no doubt.

While under questioning during the investigations, SCHWENN admitted several times that as a member of the SS during the war he and his comrades participated in the shooting of peaceful Soviet citizens on temporarily-occupied territory of the USSR.

SCHWENN in particular admitted having taken part in the shooting of forty people near the village of Shtudolichi, which was looted and burned, in the summer of 1943. SCHWENN provided detailed information about the location, the timing and the circumstances of this crime and admitted personally taking part as a machine gunner in the punishment detachment.

SCHWENN also made this admission during the trial, but stated that he had not played an active part. Residents of neighboring White Russian villages testified as witnesses at the trial and confirmed the shooting of 200 persons.

Under these circumstances it must be concluded that SCHWENN's conviction was well-founded and that his criminal activities were legally analyzed correctly.

SCHWENN is no victim of political repression and therefore is not entitled to rehabilitation.

As per the above and § § 377 and 378 of the Russian Federation's Code of Criminal Procedure, § 4b, § 9a and § 10 of the law of the RSFSR of October 18, 1991, "Concerning the Rehabilitation of Victims of Political Repression," the military court attached to Unit 16666 has decided:

Albert SCHWENN was legitimately convicted and is not subject to rehabilitation.

Affected persons or social organizations can appeal to the Military College of the Supreme Court of the Russian Federation.

Postscript

In this book I have published the memories of a man, covering about thirteen years of his life. They cover about two and a half years of active service in the *Waffen-SS* and almost eleven years as a prisoner of war held by the Soviets.

As a nineteen-year-old boy who had only just completed his basic training, he and the 1st SS Cavalry Regiment were committed to secure and pacify the General District of Zhitomir (Reich Commissariat Ukraine). In addition to the requisitioning of cattle, he experienced the burning of villages and the death of civilians.

As per the propaganda which suggested that such actions against civilians were justified, he gave little thought to whether this action was legal according to military and international law. Like millions of other soldiers on all sides, he gave no thought to disobeying these orders. Later he put the actions in the Pripyat Marshes out of his memories, not least because they were the reason for his almost eleven years as a prisoner of war. His military service therefore consisted of just basic training, one week of action at the front and his time in the SS Cavalry Replacement Battalion.

Of the approximately 400 pages of his recollections, originally only about two pages concerned this subject. It was not until my repeated inquiries about the actions in the rear area that a more accurate picture came to light. They are so important, not just because they influenced his own life until 1956, but because they are evidence of the German policy towards the USSR during the Second World War.

From left to right: Gustav Lombard, Günther Temme, and Fredo Gensicke at a reunion of former SS cavalry in 1965.

Günther Temme (born August 29, 1900) was one of the most successful German show jumpers. On December 21, 1944, he was promoted to *SS-Standartenführer der Reserve*.

Appendices

Appendix 1: History of the 8th SS Cavalry Division "Florian Geyer"

The *SS-Totenkopf-Reiter-Standarten*

As early as the end of 1934, the head of the German Army Command recorded that the *Reichsführung-SS* would be permitted to bolster police strength with up to 25,000 men from the membership of the *Allgemeine-SS*. These personnel were to have completed their compulsory military service and be between thirty-five and forty-five years old. While the SS men were serving as police reinforcements, the *Wehrmacht*'s right of disposition in the event of mobilization was suspended—the men could not be called up to serve in the army, for example.

Under the pretext of police responsibilities in the event of mobilization, there was therefore the possibility of forming an SS reserve of at least one division. As the planning envisaged transferring this potential—at least partially—into the fighting units of the SS, in 1938 the age was lowered to 25- to 35-year-old reservists.

With an eye towards expanding the SS combat units, in 1939, Hitler authorized the recruiting of volunteers with no military service for the reinforced *SS-Totenkopf-Standarten.* As these were officially designated as police reinforcements, they did not affect the allocation numbers of the armed SS units that were allowed by the *Wehrmacht.*

In the course of this expansion, orders for the formation of a mounted battalion of the reinforced *SS-Totenkopf-Standarten* were issued with effect September 15, 1939. The unit frameworks were formed within just six weeks—in particular from the cavalry *Standarte* (regiments) of the *Allgemeine-SS*—and under the command of *SS-Standartenführer* Fegelein were assigned to occupation duties in the Warsaw - Cracow - Chelmno area (*Generalgouvernement*) as the *verstärkte SS-Totenkopf-Reiter-Standarte* (Reinforced SS Death's Head Cavalry Regiment).

A *2. SS-Totenkopf-Reiter Standarte* (2nd SS Death's Head Cavalry Regiment) was formed in Lublin in the spring of 1940—again primarily from reservists of the *Allgemeine-SS*. In addition to training, the units were used to guard Polish prisoners of war and for special missions assigned by the Senior SS and Police Commander "East."

My division commander—shown here as an *SS-Standartenführer*—Hermann Fegelein.

In the course of these missions elements of the *1. SS-Totenkopf-Reiter Standarte* shot approximately 600 Polish prisoners of war on January 14, 1940.

On August 1, 1940, Hitler's and Himmler's original intention to expand the *Waffen-SS* with the reinforced *SS-Totenkopf-Standarten* manifested itself with the attachment of these units to the *Waffen-SS*. On February 25, 1941, the incorporation of the former "reinforced *SS-Totenkopf-Standarten* "was documented externally by the removal of the Death's Head collar patches and their replacement by collar patches bearing the double *Sig-Runen*. At the same time the units were renamed *SS-Kavallerie-Regimenter 1* and *2* (1st and 2nd SS Cavalry Regiments).

The *SS-Kavallerie-Brigade*

In regards to the war against the Soviet Union, on February 24, 1941, Himmler ordered the two SS cavalry regiments being employed to secure the *Generalgouvernement* combined into a brigade. On April 9, 1941, it was attached to the newly-formed *Kommandostab Reichsführer-SS* and moved into the Lyck area of East Prussia. From there, on June 26, 1941, the command staff temporarily made the 1st SS Cavalry Regiment available to the 87th Infantry Division to guard its flanks.

The SS Cavalry Brigade was then organized as follows:

- Brigade Headquarters with military police, motorcycle messenger and music platoons
- 1st SS Cavalry Regiment with 1st – 4th Troops and 5th (Heavy) Troop
- 2nd SS Cavalry Regiment with 1st – 4th Troops and 5th (Heavy) Troop
- SS Bicycle Reconnaissance Battalion with three troops
- SS Artillery Battalion with two batteries

In keeping with its original purpose, the Senior SS and Police Commander "Russia Center" also employed the SS Cavalry Brigade to "pacify" the occupied areas. In addition to combat against regular Soviet troops that had been left behind, the brigade also carried out shootings of, in particular, communists and Jews. As the temporary area of operations consisted mainly of forest and wetlands, on July 28, 1941, the "*Kommandostab Reichsführer-SS*" issued "*Guidelines for the Combing of Wetlands*":

I. Performance of Cavalry Units

(1) It must be borne in mind that the cavalry covers less distance per day than infantry without packs. A daily march performance of 25 to 37 miles is the maximum limit for the cavalry.

(2) For this reason, actions are always to be carried out so that no unnecessary distances (which would play no role for motorized forces) must be covered.

(3) Patrolling and combing, or marching with action and searching of villages, makes possible a maximum limit of 12.5 to 18.5 miles per day.

II. Police Participation

(1) The Security Police should, in principle, take part in the planning of the action. Its role is to provide reports and intelligence as the basis for planning the action.

(2) The Ordnungspolizei will take part in carrying out the actions, including patrolling, provided the necessary equipment and forces are available.

(3) Advancing simultaneously with the forces in the interior of the wetland, motorized forces of the Ordnungspolizei are to screen and cover the lateral boundary lines, tracks and roads. It should be borne in mind that an enemy wanting to break out across the roads will not come directly from the side, but will instead first flee some distance forward and then try to break out outside the area that can be combed in one day. Safeguarding the entire section, which can perhaps be combed in four days, is only necessary patrolling the roads. Stronger forces are only to be concentrated in two day sectors (37 miles).

III. Concept of Operations

(1) Each clearance action is to be carefully prepared. It must be preceded by thorough reconnaissance and scouting

Suspected partisans and requisitioning of cattle during "Operation Vistula I."

by patrols and aerial reconnaissance (if necessary by Fieseler Storch). The population is to be appropriately informed by leaflets and warned not to provide support to marauders.

(2) It is desirable to patrol as limited an area as possible, as otherwise the overview is lost.

(3) Patrolling without securing the opposite boundary of the area to be patrolled is pointless.

(4) Securing and screening the boundary are the responsibilities of the motorized and wheeled elements of the cavalry units. Security is to take the form of small hedgehog positions, as this line must be secured both in the direction of the area to be patrolled and to the rear. The roads and paths leading out of the wetland must also be guarded.

(5) Spoils living and dead (cattle) must be brought to safety.

(6) If stubborn resistance is met in the villages, it is to be overcome with the help of the air force, avoiding unnecessary casualties.

(7) Effective signals communications must be assured using all available signals equipment, so that command is always orientated. The danger that the forces may become split up and lost in the wetland must be eliminated in any event.

IV. Treatment of the Population

(1) We must be clear that the villages in the wetlands are either bases for us or bases for the enemy. They can only be bases for us if their population does not consist of criminals, rather, seen racially, of Ukrainian or some other minority population which is well-disposed towards us and hostile to the Russians or the Poles. If this is the case, then we must see to it that these villages can defend themselves against marauders and become bases for us lock, stock and barrel. Mayors are to be installed and confirmed by us. Through the Security Police, which must take part in these actions, trusted agents are to be employed at all times. The population is also to be armed to a limited degree, for otherwise, despite good intentions they will be overrun by the enemy and then their villages will serve as a source of supply for him. When villages are occupied,

> the population can best be informed of the rules of conduct by billposting. Furthermore they should be promised a share of the booty of captured partisans or marauders. Their share can be an assignment of horses (but not all), of food, carts and other things not needed by the troops.
>
> (2) If the population as a whole is seen as hostile, racially and humanly inferior or even, as is very often the case in the wetlands, composed of criminals who have settled there, all of those suspected of supporting the partisans are to be shot; women and children are to be transported away. Cattle and food are to be seized and brought to safety. The villages shall be burned to the ground.
>
> (3) Either the villages and settlements are a net of strongpoints whose residents on their own initiative kill every partisan and marauder and tell us about everything, or else they cease to exist. No enemy may find support and nourishment in this area.

After these guidelines were issued, the SS Cavalry Brigade combed the Pripyat Marshes between *Rollbahn 1* and the Pripyat River until August 11, 1941. *SS-Standartenführer* Fegelein subsequently reported that 13,788 persons had been shot. The German forces lost just two men killed. Entire villages were liquidated and in some cases burned down. Even taking into account that the SS officers (especially *SS-Standartenführer* Fegelein) boastfully exaggerated the numbers, this was still a sad action. The 2nd SS Cavalry Regiment's final report offers a depressing insight into the actions:

> **Combat impressions: none**
>
> Population: primarily Ukrainian, in second place White Russians, in third place Poles and Russians, the latter in very small numbers. Jews were mainly in the larger villages, but there they made up a high percentage of the population, in some cases from 50 to 80 percent, but in others just 25 percent.
>
> The Ukrainian and White Russian population is very cooperative. This is particularly reflected in the fact that they reported the partisan bands that were active in the area recently or some time ago. These have only been found and ferreted out in a few cases, so that they could also be shot.

Further proof of helpfulness was that the people brought milk, eggs and all sorts of food as soon as the unit moved in and made it available to the troops free and unsolicited.

Poles and Russians reserved and taciturn, however they welcomed the presence of German troops and declared that they were happy that the Bolsheviks had been driven away.

In many cases when the troops moved in, a Ukrainian custom was practiced. A table with a white tablecloth was brought out on which there was bread and salt, which were offered to the unit leaders. In one case a band was even present to welcome the troops.

Of note is the large number of children that were found in every village. It is not unusual for families to consist of ten to twelve members.

Racially the Ukrainian population makes a good impression. Though short, all are of regular form and figure with a clear facial expression. The same could also be said of the White Russians, although not as pronounced but in a similar fashion. As Poles and Russians were only present in small numbers, their characteristics were not identified.

Soil conditions: The entire area consists of large wetlands with scattered sandy areas, so that the soil is not very suitable for agriculture. If it is better in a few places, it is also poorer in others.

The area is traversed by many canals and streams, a few of which are regulated, however the vast majority flow unregulated. Between them are vast forests, consisting largely of birch, alder and pine.

The principal crops are rye, hay and potatoes. Everywhere in-between hemp and flax; there is also a great deal of millet, which is of great importance as a food. Hemp and flax is grown to satisfy the local requirement for fabrics. Almost all of the clothing is home-spun or hand-woven. That of the Ukrainian population is also embroidered.

The road conditions were extremely bad, part sandy, part muddy, so that the troop supply trains often had to remain two days behind the troops.

Action in the Pripyat Marshes.

Supply: Because of the extremely poor road conditions, the delivery of food and oats was particularly difficult. Shortages of food were made up for by voluntary donations from the inhabitants. Only oats for the horses could not be found anywhere. Hay also could not be obtained, so that the horses had to be fed almost exclusively on grass. A disadvantage of the poor delivery of rations and oats was that the mounted battalion had been assigned a sector to pacify that was too big. In some cases a baggage train of twenty to twenty-five panye wagons was formed so that the troops could carry everything with them. The greatest supply difficulties were encountered by the 3rd Troop, which was deployed in the southern areas, south of the Pripyat.

Condition of the Troops: The state of health of the troops was very good throughout the entire time of the action. Only a very few of the men needed to be sent to hospital, but after several days they were able to rejoin their units. The morale of the troops was very good throughout.

Condition of the Horses: The condition of the horses suffered because of insufficient supplies of oats and the strenuous marches which had to be made daily. If, for example, an area 18.5 miles deep had to be pacified, this meant 37 or more miles for horse and rider. A large number of horses were lost to action in this way, through lameness, pressure damage, and among the draught horses withers pressure and chafing. Some horses had to be replaced by farm horses. The men covered long distances on foot to take the pressure off the horses. The 2nd and 4th Troops suffered the greatest number of horses lost to action.

Pacification: Pacification followed the following procedure: the unit commander or platoon leader met with the mayor of the affected village and discussed all questions concerning the population. He was asked about the number and composition of the inhabitants, whether they were Ukrainian or Russian etc. He was also asked if there were still Communists in the village, or disguised Red Army personnel or anyone else who had been an active Bolshevik. Usually residents then reported having seen partisan bands or otherwise suspicious persons.

> If such elements were still in the village they were arrested and after a brief interrogation were released or shot. Where there was no order service, one was set up, taking into account the ethnic makeup of the village. In small villages the order service was placed under the mayor. He was forbidden to undertake any political activity.
>
> Jewish looters were shot. Only a few craftsmen, working in Wehrmacht repair shops, were left behind. Driving women and children into the swamps did not have the desired effect, for the swamps were not deep enough for them to sink into. Solid ground (probably sand) was reached after a depth of three feet, so that sinking was not possible.
>
> No Communists were encountered. In most cases there were persons who had acted as Communists. Reports about partisan bands were in most cases exaggerated. Searches were usually fruitless. In one case a Polish priest was shot because he made propaganda for Poland and encouraged the population to hold out: Poland would rise again. Leaflets with a similar message were dropped in the area of Kamien Koscyrsko.
>
> Ukrainian priests were very ready to help and made themselves available during every action. It was also striking that the vast majority of the population spoke highly of the Jewish component of the population. They did, however, help in the rounding up of the Jews.
>
> The total number of looters shot by the mounted battalion was: 6,526 people.
>
> About ten prisoners were taken. One Russian agent is still in custody at battalion headquarters in Luniniec.
>
> To sum up, it can be said that the action can be characterized as a success.

From August 15–30, 1941, followed the combing of the area south of the Pripyat between Turov and Mozyr. From there the SS Cavalry Brigade marched into the triangular area between the Pripyat in the southwest, the Dniepr in the east, and the Mozyr to Gomel rail line in the north.

Burning down villages suspected of supporting partisans.

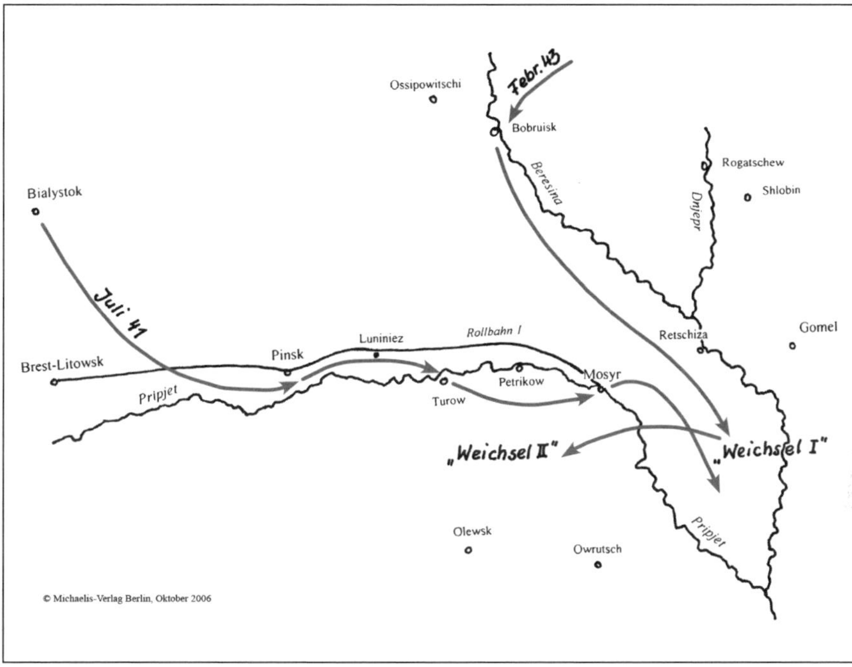

Map: Area of operations in the summer of 1941 and spring of 1943.

Action in the Rzhev Area

At the beginning of October 1941, the SS Cavalry Brigade was ordered about 310 miles to the north, into the Toropets–Cholm area, and attached to the commander of Rear Army Area Center. On October 18, 1941, the 1st SS Cavalry Regiment carried out a pacification action along the Velikiye–Luki and Rzhev rail line.

The Soviets launched their winter offensive on December 5, 1941. They crossed the Volga between Lake Seliger and the area north of Rzhev and placed the German 9th Army in a very serious situation. The German XXIII Army Corps was encircled west of Olenino. Without winter clothing, cold-weather lubricants for weapons and equipment, and shortages of food and ammunition, in temperatures as low as minus forty degrees the German troops could offer little resistance.

The SS Cavalry Brigade was finally sent towards Rzhev to bolster the threatened units. The SS Bicycle Reconnaissance Battalion was

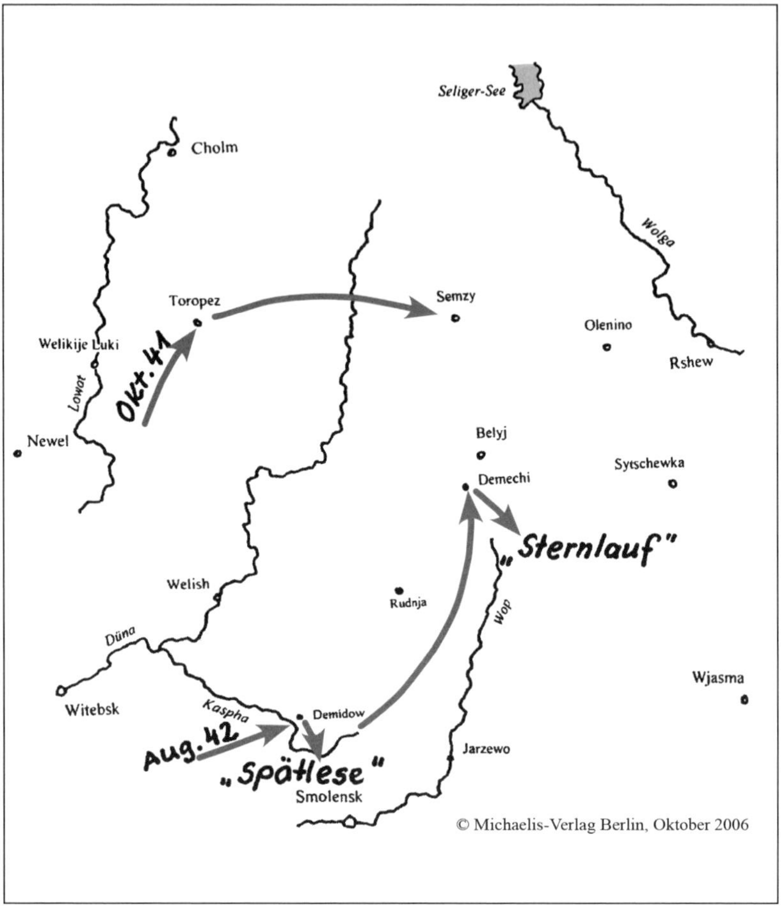

Map: The area of operations in autumn-winter 1941–42 and summer-winter 1943.

the first unit to go, and on December 14, 1941, it was ordered into the sector held by the 253rd Infantry Division. The two cavalry regiments followed at the end of December. They were deployed in the XXIII Army Corps' sector and were attached to the 206th Infantry Division. On January 11, 1942, there was a brief letup in the enemy pressure, however powerful enemy forces drove far to the southwest and reached the area northwest of Vyazma. The German counterattack began on January 22, 1942, and the next day the main line of resistance was again closed.

Members of the SS Cavalry Brigade in the winter of 1941–42.

SS-Standartenführer Fegelein decorates members of the SS Cavalry Brigade (winter 1941–42).

After the end of the Soviet winter offensive the SS Cavalry Brigade remained in its positions west of Rzhev and was sporadically used against straggling enemy elements. In mid-April 1942, the unit was pulled out of the front and was sent to SS Training Camp Heidelager for expansion into a division. A battalion-strength battle group under the command of *SS-Sturmbannführer* Zehender initially remained behind in the main line of resistance. Battle Group Zehender followed to Debica at the end of June 1942.

The SS Cavalry Division

Following an agreement with Hungary concerning the recruiting of ethnic Germans for the *Waffen-SS*, in the spring of 1942, the force acquired more than 16,000 men to use as replacements. This enabled the *SS-Führungshauptamt* to make good the personnel losses sustained in the winter of 1941–42. There were insufficient numbers of Reich German volunteers to meet the need for personnel. It also enabled the SS Cavalry Brigade to be expanded into the SS Cavalry Division. The remaining approximately 3,000 men were joined at Training Camp Heidelager in Debica (*Generalgouvernement*) by a total of about 9,000 ethnic Germans from Hungary.

After *SS-Standartenführer* Fegelein was named *Waffen-SS* liaison officer in Führer Headquarters, *SS-Brigadeführer* Bittrich took over command of the new division. While the new units formed from the ethnic German recruits stayed at the training camp, already in mid-August 1942, operational units were ordered sent back to the 9th Army.

Attached to the 330th Infantry Division in the area held by LIX Army Corps, the units first took part in "Operation Spätlese," which finished on September 20, 1942. The operation was directed against straggling Red Army units and partisans in the area of forest and wetlands west of Yarzevo. Then the units marched to the front and occupied positions between the 197th and 330th Infantry Divisions at the seam between XXIII and LIX Army Corps in the Demechi area.

In mid-October, the units still at Debica were transferred to the front. Most of the ethnic Germans had received adequate training which lasted about six months. At the beginning of November 1942, the 1st SS Cavalry Regiment reinforced by an anti-tank platoon and a 20 mm flak platoon was in the Kurocha–Novo Pokrovskoyino–Baturino–Padsaychevo area and its orders were to reconnoiter the Lozmyanka River line and guard the right flank of VI Army Corps. The 2nd SS Cavalry Regiment was assigned to the 4th Parachute Regiment in the Osotkya sector, while the 3rd SS Cavalry Regiment, just coming from the Generalgouvernement, was to make contact with the 197th Infantry Division in the Kletki–Rasinkova area. The SS Bicycle Reconnaissance Battalion occupied the Stary Dvor area, while the SS Pioneer Battalion fortified positions in the Nikala–Yedrivichi–Velyushino area. The SS Signals Battalion was quartered in Nekuyudova and laid field telephone lines between the units of the SS Cavalry Division.

On November 25, 1942, the Red Army launched an offensive in four places: northwest of Sychevka, west of Rzhev and north and south of Belye. By about 1400, enemy forces had taken Toropino (6.2 miles southeast of Belye), Yemelyanova, Petruchina and Zyguni and were advancing on the road to Demechi. The 1st SS Cavalry Regiment, which was army reserve, was subsequently sent into the Belousovo area (11.8 miles southwest of Belye) and in the evening was moved further forward toward Belye. The Soviet troops drove to Demechi, where their advance was halted. The next day the enemy established himself in Selishche, between the 2nd Luftwaffe Field Division and the 197th Infantry Division. Although the town was retaken, the enemy succeeded in expanding his penetration to a depth of 12.5 miles. On November 28, 1942, *SS-Brigadeführer* Bittner gave the reinforced 1st and 2nd SS Cavalry Regiments their battle orders. XXX Army Corps under *General der Artillerie* Fretter-Pico was withdrawn from Army Group North and moved into the sector. The next day the SS Cavalry Division was attached to XXX Army Corps.

The German counterattack began on December 7, 1942. The 20th Infantry Division, 19th Panzer Division and the SS Cavalry Division advanced from the north, while elements of the 1st Panzer Division and the Fusilier Regiment *"Großdeutschland"* came from the south. The combat units suffered casualties of about 50% in one month, however on December 10, 1942, contact was established with XXXXI Panzer Corps (*General der Panzertruppe* Harpe). The 1st and 19th Panzer Divisions linked up, encircling a large enemy force.

Members of the SS Cavalry Division in the winter of 1942–43.

Fallen Soviet soldiers.

The effort to destroy these troops began on December 11, 1942. One week later, the SS Cavalry Division, with a strength of 310 officers and 10,569 other ranks, was attached to XXXXI Panzer Corps. The 1st and 3rd SS Cavalry Regiments were pulled out of the front and transferred to rest areas. The 2nd SS Cavalry Regiment along with the SS Bicycle Reconnaissance Battalion and the SS Artillery Regiment remained in action against partisans and straggling Red Army troops from the previous battle with elements of the 20th Panzer Division in the Nefedova–Lykino and Demechi areas. On December 23, 1942, the SS Bicycle Reconnaissance Battalion discovered three partisan units with a strength of about 3,000 men in a wooded area south of Soino. The partisans even had a small airfield.

On January 4, 1943, XXXXI Panzer Corps ordered the pacification of the area north and south of the road to Nikitinka. The 3rd SS Cavalry Regiment and the SS Bicycle Reconnaissance Battalion were initially assigned reconnaissance tasks. The area (about 116 square miles) consisted mainly of swamp primeval forest. There were several partisan groups operating there, including the Chapayev, Yakovlev, Korevsky, Morgov, Vorodpokov and Voroshilov Brigades.

At the same time, *SS-Brigadeführer* Bittrich handed command of the division over to *SS-Standartenführer* Freitag. Bittrich, an outstanding tactician, was given command of the *SS-Panzer-Grenadier-Division "Hohenstaufen."*

Under *SS-Standartenführer* Freitag's command, approximately 3,000 SS cavalry took part in "Operation *Sternlauf*" in the area of the Vop River from January 27 to February 8, 1943. *General der Panzertruppe* Harpe and *Generaloberst* Model help plan the operation, which was supposed to lead to the encirclement and destruction of the partisans in the forest south of Tatyanka.

On February 14, 1943, the SCD left the XXXXI Panzer Corps, was ordered to the Bobruisk area approximately 250 miles away, and again attached to the Senior SS and Police Commander Russia Center.

On February 16, 1943, orders were issued for the formation of a regiment-strength battle group, which was to be deployed in the Dmitrovsk area (approximately fifty-six miles southwest of Orel) with XXXXVII Panzer Corps. The 2nd Panzer Army was hard pressed as a result of the Red Army's winter offensive. Battle Group Zehender marched to Komarichi (southwest of Dmitrovsk). There was extremely fierce fighting there until mid-March. On March 24, 1943, Headquarters 2nd Panzer Army ordered the subsequent engagement of the partisans in the forests south of Briansk–Navlya (approximately twenty-five miles northwest of Dmitrovsk), which had been reinforced by Red Army troops. On April 5, 1943, SS Battle Group Zehender was ordered back to Lapichi (northwest of Bobruisk).

After *SS-Standartenführer* Freitag had shown little agility during the division's actions, several weeks later on April 20, 1943, Himmler relieved him of command and installed *SS-Oberführer* Fegelein as the new division commander, promoting him to *SS-Brigadeführer*.

Action Against Partisans in the Reich Commissariat Ukraine

About two weeks later followed the action in the area between the Pripyat in the southwest, the Dniepr in the east and the Mozyr to Gomel rail line in the north. The SS cavalry had previously been deployed there from August 15–30, 1941. After talks with *General der Infanterie* von Schenkendorf, commander of the rear army area, and *SS-Obergruppenführer* von dem Bach, the "*Reichsführer-SS*' Plenipotentiary for Anti-Partisan Operations," on May 9, 1943, the SS Cavalry Division was ordered to take part in "Operation Vistula I."

The units advanced south and were supposed to clear the area to the Choiniki–Bragin road of the strong partisan units thought to be there. The following partisan groups were thought to be in the so-called "Wet Triangle":

- Elements of the main Kolpak Group with headquarters in Grebenovo, fortified camp in Lesnoye, main camp in Omelkovshchin, strength approximately 600 men.
- Sanyukhov Group, headquarters in Raysk (15.5 miles south of Saspa), recruited mainly from regular troops of the Soviet 44th Rifle Regiment. Strength was about 500 men who had access to German uniforms, especially those of the *Luftwaffe*.
- Kolpak Group, strength up to 10,000 men (!) operated south of the line Lotscha (sixty miles south of Rechiza), Savichi, Babchin, Tulgovichi (twelve miles south of Choiniki). Supply

battalion and an airfield in the forest west of Drunki. Band headquarters in Novy Radin.
- Filipenko Group, headquarters in Stepanov, in the south of the "Wet Triangle."

On May 12, 1943, during the initial reconnaissance operations, there was fighting between the reinforced SS Reconnaissance Battalion and a roughly 600-man-strong partisan group. The next day 500 partisan vehicles were captured in a forest.

From left to right: Günther Temme, Hermann Fegelein, and Gustav Lombard during "Operation Vistula II" in the summer of 1943.

With respect to the action and his return as commanding officer, two days later *SS-Brigadeführer* Fegelein issued the following order of the day to the SS Cavalry Division:

> The tasks the division has been given have been ordered by the *Führer*, because they are decisive for the firming up and strengthening of the entire front in the east. It is an honor for our unit to now prove that through our superiority of command and through stubborn determination we are in the position—both in the march and in combat performance—to destroy the dangerous foe facing us. Our will to destroy must be implacable, without mercy or compassion. Any softness will mean a lengthening of the war. With precisely the same impetus and momentum and the same determination with once I led the *Schutzstaffel*'s first cavalry *Sturm* [company], I assume command of the Greater German Army's only cavalry unit. Long live the *Führer*!

From left to right: *SS-Obersturmbannführer* Temme, *SS-Brigadeführer* Fegelein, and *SS-Standartenführer* Lombard.

Fegelein, Temme, and Lombard interrogate Ukrainian civilians.

No decisive success was achieved in the difficult terrain of forest and swamp, however. On June 10, 1943, the SS Cavalry Division returned to its starting positions. The operation had, however, resulted in the acquisition of valuable agricultural goods. Requisitioned in the area were:

5,676 cattle
1,073 calves
1,233 horses
3,153 sheep
1,398 pigs

Following the operation, the SS Cavalry Division moved from Army Group Center's rear area to the rear area of Army Group South and thus from the area of the Senior SS and Police Commander Russia Center into that of the Senior SS and Police Commander Russia South, *SS-Obergruppenführer* Prützmann in Kiev.

There the SS cavalry were to take on the approximately 10,000 partisans in the area of Ovruch–Mozyr–Petrikov–Leltshitsy–Olovsk–Belekurichi–Ovruch in "Operation Vistula II." Crossing the Pripyat River between Skrygalova and Petrikov, fast forces of the SS Cavalry Division were to attack along the Ubort River. Police Battle Group Schimana (without the SS Cavalry Division) was to march into the named area from Ovelak. The Royal Hungarian VII Army Corps and SS Grenadier Replacement Battalion East were deployed around Ovruch to prevent the partisan groups from breaking through to the south and east.

On July 19, 1943, the SS Cavalry Division was able to encircle and destroy a strong partisan group. Partisan losses in this operation were 1,256 killed and 206 captured. The SS cavalry's casualties were one officer, seven non-commissioned officers and fourteen enlisted men killed, and fifty-six men wounded. The relationship shows that the enemy dead probably included numerous unarmed civilians.

In the following days the units were employed primarily to guard the harvest. Smaller engagements with National-Ukrainian partisans showed that, in contrast to the communist-orientated partisans, they preferred to carry out attacks on economic installations than direct actions against the German occupation forces.

Action at the Front in the Merefa–Mishurin-Rog–Kirovograd Area

Even during the failed German summer offensive ("Operation Citadel") the Red Army itself took the offensive and drove towards Kharkov. The SS Cavalry Division subsequently received orders to transfer from the Mozyr area approximately 310 miles to the east into the Merefa area (south of Kharkov). On August 21, 1943, the unit reached the XXXXII Army Corps (8th Army) and was deployed on the boundary with the LVII Panzer Corps (1st Panzer Army). The chaotic conditions that developed in the following weeks were not due to the unit's manpower, which was about 30% below authorized strength, rather they resulted from the fact that the SS Cavalry Division had not been conceived for large-scale mobile warfare against an armored enemy.

XXXXII Army Corps made preparations to cross to the west bank of the Dniepr. On August 26, 1943, after a heavy artillery bombardment, Soviet armored units attacked and achieved deep penetrations, especially into the division's open flank. In fierce defensive fighting the self-propelled guns of the SS Artillery Regiment prevented the worst. Individual elements of the division were encircled. Forming all-round defense positions, they held on, in some cases for more than eighteen hours. Scratch units were able to fight their way to the units and a weak continuous main line of resistance was established.

At the beginning of September 1943, the SS cavalry were attached to LII Army Corps. The units conducted a difficult and costly fighting retreat from the northern Donets near Cherk–Bishkin southwest to the Dniepr, which they reached on September 25, 1943. There they were attached to LVII Panzer Corps in the Mishurin-Rog area. A thin defense line was established held by men on the verge of exhaustion. Two days later the first Soviet infantry units crossed the Dniepr and established a bridgehead south of Mishurin-Rog. The SS Cavalry Division was among the units which tried unsuccessfully to eliminate the bridgehead. SS cavalry were initially successful in repulsing Soviet attacks from the bridgehead northwest to Kommunar and southwest to Lichovka–Vladimirovka–Konstantinovka.

At the end of the month the units of the *Waffen-SS* were numbered consecutively. The units of the cavalry division were numbered as follows:

8th SS Cavalry Division
15th SS Cavalry Regiment
16th SS Cavalry Regiment
17th SS Cavalry Regiment

Division units were also assigned the number 8.

After the positions between Kremenchug and Mishurin-Rog had to be given up, the 8th SS Cavalry Division withdrew into the Kirovograd–Krivoy-Rog area. On October 27, 1943, it launched a counterattack near Zapadenka. Numerically far superior enemy forces with tank support had broken into the German main line of resistance. Rapidly-formed battle groups were able to intercept and seal off the Soviet attack.

On November 5, 1943, fighting began for possession of Vasilyevka. The German defenders fought stubbornly and Soviet bombers destroyed their positions. Soviet superiority in men and material was overwhelming. Three days later the 8th SS Cavalry Division was attached to XI Panzer Corps.

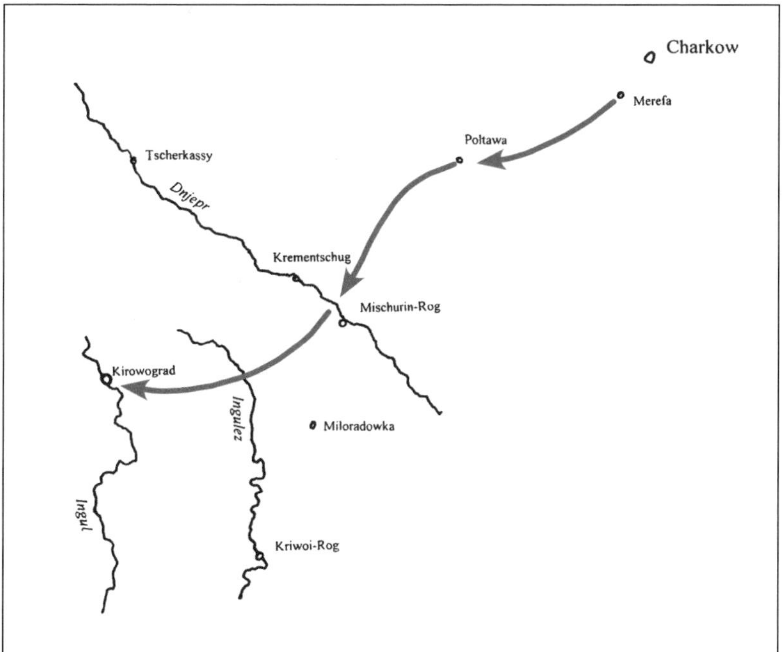

Another day of large-scale fighting took place on November 15, 1943, when more than 200 enemy tanks and powerful infantry units attacking after heavy artillery preparation. The last reserves were committed and the front held. Five days later the division was again attached to LVII Panzer Corps.

On November 21, 1943, the Red Army attacked again, following an intense artillery bombardment. In ice and snow the troops, whose fighting strength was often just fifteen to twenty men, repulsed the enemy. One week later enemy troops succeeded in breaking into the 8th SS Cavalry Division's left flank near the Bashitanka Gorge. Self-propelled guns of the 8th SS Artillery Regiment also eliminated this penetration.

The attempt by the 3rd Ukrainian Front to bring about the collapse of the 1st Panzer Army's positions was initially unsuccessful: Krivoy-Rog and Zaporozhye were held.

Rehabilitation in Croatia

After the division was virtually destroyed in these actions, on December 8, 1943, Himmler agreed with the head of the *Wehrmacht* Operations Staff that the 8th SS Cavalry Division should be rehabilitated as quickly as possible. On December 21, 1943, the 8th SS Reconnaissance Battalion and the 16th SS Cavalry Regiment were withdrawn from the front and sent to Esseg (Croatia) for rehabilitation. The remaining units remained with XXXXVII Army Corps as SS Battle Group Lombard and followed to Croatia in January 1944.

While the 17th SS Cavalry Regiment was deployed at Kovel, rehabilitation of the 8th SS Cavalry Division, at least in personnel, was carried out using Reich and ethnic German replacements. On March 12, 1944, Hitler awarded the cavalry unit the name "Florian Geyer." The 8th SS Cavalry Division "Florian Geyer" was organized as follows:

15th SS Cavalry Regiment, with 6 troops
16th SS Cavalry Regiment, with 6 troops
17th SS Cavalry Regiment, with 6 troops
8th Motorized Artillery Regiment
8th SS Armored Reconnaissance Battalion
8th SS Pioneer Battalion

The May 1944 issue of the illustrated magazine *Reichskriegerzeitung* propagandized the increased use of cavalry. It urged the veterans of the First World War to urge their sons, "to stay true to their fathers' glorious branch of service and to volunteer." In fact this showed that the shortages of oil and steel were already seriously handicapping the use of motorized and armored units.

„Achtung Kavallerie!"

Wir alten Reiter, wir Kürassiere, Dragoner, Husaren, Jäger zu Pferde horchen auf: die Kavallerie lebt noch! Aus dem Rundfunk schallten beim Verlesen des OKW.-Berichts zu wiederholten Malen Sätze an unsere Ohren, in denen von erfolgreichen Unternehmungen unserer Kavallerie-Verbände, aber auch von Massenangriffen sowjetischer Kavallerie-Verbände die Rede war.

Bereits in den Jahren des Wiederaufbaues der Wehrmacht hatte so mancher unter uns von jungen Kameraden seines Traditionsregimentes auf die Frage: „Was machen die Pferde?" die Antwort bekommen: „Pferde? Panzer meinen Sie wohl!" Und dann hatten wir gesehen, daß die Biesen an seiner Mütze und um seine Schulterstücke nicht das „Gelb" der Kavallerie, sondern das „Rosa" der Panzertruppe zeigten. Wir erfuhren aus der Presse, in Sonderheit aus Fachaufsätzen in der „Reichskriegerzeitung", daß im Westen Europas mit seinem engmaschigen, gut ausgebauten Straßennetz die Kavallerie so gut wie verschwunden sei, daß z. B. England nur noch ein paar Parade-Regimenter zu Pferde habe, daß aber, je weiter man nach dem wegearmen Osten käme, desto stärker der Anteil der Kavallerie im Heere geblieben sei, um endlich im Sowjetischen noch fast ein Drittel der Gesamtstärke auszumachen. Wie weit damals bereits im großdeutschen Heere die Umwandlung der berittenen in motorisierte Truppen gediehen war, blieb uns aus begreiflichen Gründen verborgen. Heute wissen wir, daß noch bestanden: drei Reiter-Regimenter, die bei der Mobilmachung zu einer Kavallerie-Division zusammengefaßt, und eine Anzahl Kavallerie-Regimenter, die zu dem gleichen Termin in Aufklärungs-Abteilungen aufgespalten wurden.

Wir waren uns aus unseren Weltkriegserfahrungen heraus — ganz besonders, wenn wir die großen Attacken von Haelen, Lagarde oder Borsymie mitgeritten hatten — klar darüber, daß die Tage geschlossener Angriffe zu Pferde, mit der Lanze, den Degen in der Faust, im Zeichen der vernichtenden Feuerwirkung neuzeitlicher Maschinenwaffen endgültig vorüber seien. Wir sahen die Aufgaben der Kavallerie mit den Augen eines ihrer begeistertsten Vorkämpfer aus dem Hunderttausendmann-Heer, der die Sätze prägte: „Die Kavallerie ist berufen, ihre Feuerwaffen über jedes Gelände hinweg rasch und überraschend an den entscheidenden Punkten des Schlachtfeldes zur Wirkung zu bringen. Sie reitet, um zu schießen, und sie schießt, um zu reiten, d. h. um im sprungweisen Vorwärtsgehen dem Feinde mit ihrem Feuer an der Klinge zu bleiben. Sie muß hierzu mit Maschinenwaffen (Maschinengewehren und Geschützen) gesättigt sein."

Im gegenwärtigen Kriege hat sich nun die Kavallerie überall dort bewährt, wo ihre Organisation, das Gelände und die Feindlage dieser ihrer Eigenart entgegenkamen: in den Sand- und Sumpfsteppen des Ostens, in Kampfräumen mit weitmaschigem Verteidigungsnetz, auf der Verfolgung, beim Decken des Rückzuges, beim Ausfüllen von Kampflücken. Auch im raschen Überwinden von Wasserläufen ohne Brücken und Fähren tat sie sich hervor, ebenso im überraschenden Zerstören von Flußbrücken und anderen Kunstbauten des Verkehrsnetzes. Die Aufklärungsabteilungen erwarben sich hohe Verdienste, indem sie das Bild, das die Luft- und die motorisierte Erdaufklärung von der Feindlage entworfen hatten, durch ihre Nah- und Gefechtsaufklärung weitgehend ergänzten.

Der deutschen Kavallerie-Division war unter anderem die schnelle Überwindung des Narew im Polenfeldzug, die Besetzung Hollands und die Abriegelung der Lagerfestung Paris zu danken. Die rumänische Kavallerie hat sich in den Feldzügen gegen die Sowjets besonders im Don- und Dnjepr-Bogen hervorgetan, die italienische Kavallerie hat sogar eine erfolgreiche Attacke gegen bolschewistische Infanterie geritten.

Die Sowjets haben ihre Kavallerie sehr stark eingesetzt und machen viel Rühmens von ihren Erfolgen, unterschlagen aber, daß sie dann stets den Kürzeren zog, wenn sie auf kampfkräftige deutsche Widersacher traf. Den Sowjets kommt zugute, daß sie als Ersatz für ihre Kavallerie über eine Jugend verfügen, die von Kindesbeinen an mit dem Pferde vertraut ist. Bei ihrer Ausbildung in der Truppe suchen die Sowjets die Überlieferungen der Reiterei des zaristischen Heeres, vor allem der in ihm einst vertretenen Reitervölker der

ϟϟ-Reiter durchqueren einen Fluß

Oststeppen, der Kosaken, Kirgisen, Kalmüc und Tataren, mit den Forderungen neuzeitlic Waffentechnik zu vereinen. Die von Natur oft scheinbaren, struppigen, aber abgehärteten Pf werden geschult, dem abgesessenen Reiter Schritt und Tritt zu folgen, sich auf Zuruf

Kamerad Pferd

Von Oberst a. D. P. Buhle.

Seit 1914, nun rund 30 Jahre lang, ringt Deutschland um seinen nationalen und völkischen Bestand, sowie um die Erhaltung der deutschen und europäischen Kulturgüter. In zwei Weltkriegen

Hitler awarded the name "Florian Geyer" to the 8th SS Cavalry Division on March 12, 1944, after which appropriate cuff titles were issued. These were worn on the left cuff of the SS field blouse.

8th SS Anti-Tank Battalion
8th SS Assault Gun Battalion
8th SS Motorized Signals Battalion
8th SS Anti-Aircraft Battalion
8th SS Veterinary Company
8th SS Medical Battalion
8th SS Economic Battalion

To create a more employable frontline division, more emphasis was placed on motorization and the provision of heavy weapons. Order for the assault guns battery to be expanded into a battalion could not be carried out, however.

Action at Kovel

While the division was being brought up to strength at Essig with about 3,000 replacements, the 17th SS Cavalry Regiment, which had been newly formed at SS Training Camp Heidelager and which had been used for a time against Polish partisans, received orders to move to Kovel. There the Red Army had succeeded in driving through the main line of resistance between the 2nd Army and 4th Panzer Army, opening a breach ninety-three miles wide. As the area consisted mainly of swamp, the threat existed that the enemy might be able to advance quickly through the transport hub of Kovel into the Generalgouvernement.

The 17th SS Cavalry Regiment entrained on January 16, 1944. It was attached to the von dem Bach Group and committed near Kolki on the Styr River (43.5 miles east of Kovel). The first encounters with regular Soviet troops took place on January 29 and 31, 1944, and partial penetrations into the German main line of resistance were eliminated. On February 9, the regiment attacked and retook the town of Rossysze on the Styr River. On February 22, the attack was continued across the Styr with members of the 7th Panzer Division, and XXXXVII Panzer Corps gained important information about enemy strength. Interestingly, it was discovered that large numbers of partisans were at the front with regular troops.

At the beginning of March 1944, the 17th SS Cavalry Regiment was moved into the area northeast of the Kovel to Povursk rail line. The length of the area to be secured meant that the regiment could only hold a series of strongpoints. It began operations with thirty-one officers, however only six remained with the troops—the rest had been killed or wounded in the past six weeks. On March 14, 1944, there was fierce defensive fighting. Two days later *SS-Obergruppenführer* von dem Bach, overwhelmed by the task of defending Kovel and ill, was relieved by *SS-Gruppenführer* Gille. Kovel was designated a "fortified place" and on March 17, 1944, it was encircled by the Soviets.

On March 30, 1944, German troops began the relief of Kovel. Elements of the 5th Jäger (Light Infantry) Division and the 4th and 5th Panzer Divisions were able to break through the Soviet positions on the western and southwestern pocket fronts. The almost 2,000 wounded inside the pocket were first to be evacuated. *General der Infanterie* Hoßbach, commanding general of LVI Panzer Corps, assumed command and his task was to widen the narrow corridor into Kovel and provide adequate protection for it. Fighting to drive the enemy troops from the city and establish a firm main line of resistance went on until the end of April 1944. The 17th SS Cavalry Regiment was subsequently taken out of action and moved to the Kisber area in Hungary. There it formed the core of the new 22nd SS Volunteer Cavalry Division.

The Occupation of Hungary and Action in Transylvania

During the occupation of Hungary on March 19, 1944 ("Operation Margarethe"), duty in Croatia consisted of training the recruits and securing the area against partisans. During the Hungarian operation the 8th SS Cavalry Division "Florian Geyer," under the command of *SS-Oberführer* Streckenbach, moved into the area along the Danube between Mohács and Duna–Földvár.

Effective April 1, 1944, *SS-Obersturmbannführer* Rumohr was placed in command of the division. *SS-Oberführer* Streckenbach took over the 19th SS Volunteer Grenadier Division (Latvian No. 2). The cavalry division saw no combat—instead the men enjoyed a relatively pleasant stay in the ethnic German areas.

While many German combat units which had taken part in the occupation were soon withdrawn from Hungary and sent to the hard-pressed Eastern Front, the SS cavalry remained in the security area until summer 1944. Following the collapse of the front in

Rumania, on August 20, 1944, the division command received orders to proceed to Transylvania. The units had been trained for almost nine months and together with the men with Eastern Front experience formed a capable combat unit.

On the night of August 23–24, 1944, the *Wehrmacht* Operations Staff ordered that *General der Infanterie* von Greiffenberg, the general in command in Hungary, was to bring the 8th SS Cavalry Division "Florian Geyer" to march readiness. This was one of the measures taken by the German side in reaction to the political change in Rumania.

After an audience with the Rumanian King Michael, on August 23, 1944, the Rumanian head of state, Marshall Antonescu, was arrested, and a ceasefire was announced with America, Great Britain and the USSR. Hitler planned to put down the putsch, but a lack of forces made this impossible. The Rumanian Army was subordinated to the Red Army and turned against the Germans.

At the beginning of September the division was transferred to Rumania. After a 310-mile rail journey, the SS Cavalry Division was attached to *SS-Obergruppenführer* Phleps, the Senior SS and Police Commander Transylvania. The affected units took up defensive positions on the northwestern bank of the Marosch River immediately after detraining in the Neumarkt (Tàrgu Mures in Rumanian) area. The sector held by the 8th SS Cavalry Division "Florian Geyer" was between Neumarkt and Ludus to its southwest and was approximately thirty-one miles in length. From the positions on the hills north of the Marosch, the view extended from the barren, mainly treeless slopes far across the winding valley. This made it possible to quickly identify and engage enemy attacks. In the days that followed there was heavy rain and fierce battles against attacking enemy troops. On September 20, 1944, the division was attached to XXIX Army Corps.

When the Red Army, including Rumanian units, launched a major offensive on October 6, 1944, the 8th SS Cavalry Division "Florian Geyer" covered the XXIX Army Corps' withdrawal to the northwest. Numerous straggling *Wehrmacht* units were integrated into the division and remained with the SS units until the end in Budapest. The two motorized units (8th SS Armored Reconnaissance Battalion and 8th SS Pioneer Battalion) formed the rear guard. Three days later the *Wehrmacht* communiqué reported:

> The 8th SS Cavalry Division, under the command of Knight's Cross holder *SS-Standartenführer* Rumohr and made up largely of Germans from southeastern Europe, has fought magnificently in the battles in Transylvania!

The End in Hungary

On October 10–11, 1944, the 8th SS Cavalry Division withdrew northwest to Bontida. There the 2nd Ukrainian Front had achieved deep penetrations against the Hungarian 25th Infantry Division and the 9th Reserve Division east of Klausenburg. Between October 12–16, 1944, the retreat led further in a northwest direction to Marghita (approximately seventy-five miles northwest of Klausenburg), with the two motorized units still covering the withdrawing forces.

On October 21, 1944, the High Command of Army Group South, ordered Army Group Wöhler, under which was XXIX Army Corps, to withdraw behind the Theiss River. The next day the 8th SS Cavalry Division "Florian Geyer" withdrew into the area south of Nagy Karoly (northeast of Debrecen). From October 23, 1944, the SS cavalry were already in a 12.5-mile sector of front south of Nyiregyhaza. Together with the 1st Panzer Division, the 15th and 18th SS Cavalry Regiments repulsed heavy Soviet infantry attacks west of Hajdunanas and Hajdudorog. Three days later Nyiregyhaza was retaken in a counterattack with the 3rd Mountain Division and the 23rd Panzer Division. The German forces subsequently withdrew to the south. On October 27, 1944, the 8th SS Armored Reconnaissance Battalion, reinforced by quad anti-aircraft guns (*Vierlingsflak*), was briefly attached to the 4th Mountain Division and committed to the attack along the Nyiregyhaz–Ujfeherto rail line.

Two days later the 8th SS Cavalry Division "Florian Geyer" left the area south of Nyiregyhaza and on November 1, 1944, crossed the Theiss River, about 18.5 miles distant. The SS cavalry regiments moved into the Miskolc area, with the 15th SS Cavalry Regiment and the 8th SS Artillery Regiment continuing southwest in the direction of Budapest. The 8th SS Armored Reconnaissance Battalion crossed the Theiss at Tiszalöc (east of Tiszakeszi) and marched to Tiszakeszi. There it occupied a bridgehead position.

Attached to *Korpsgruppe* (Corps Group) *Breith*, at the beginning of November 1944 the division, together with the *Panzergrenadier-*

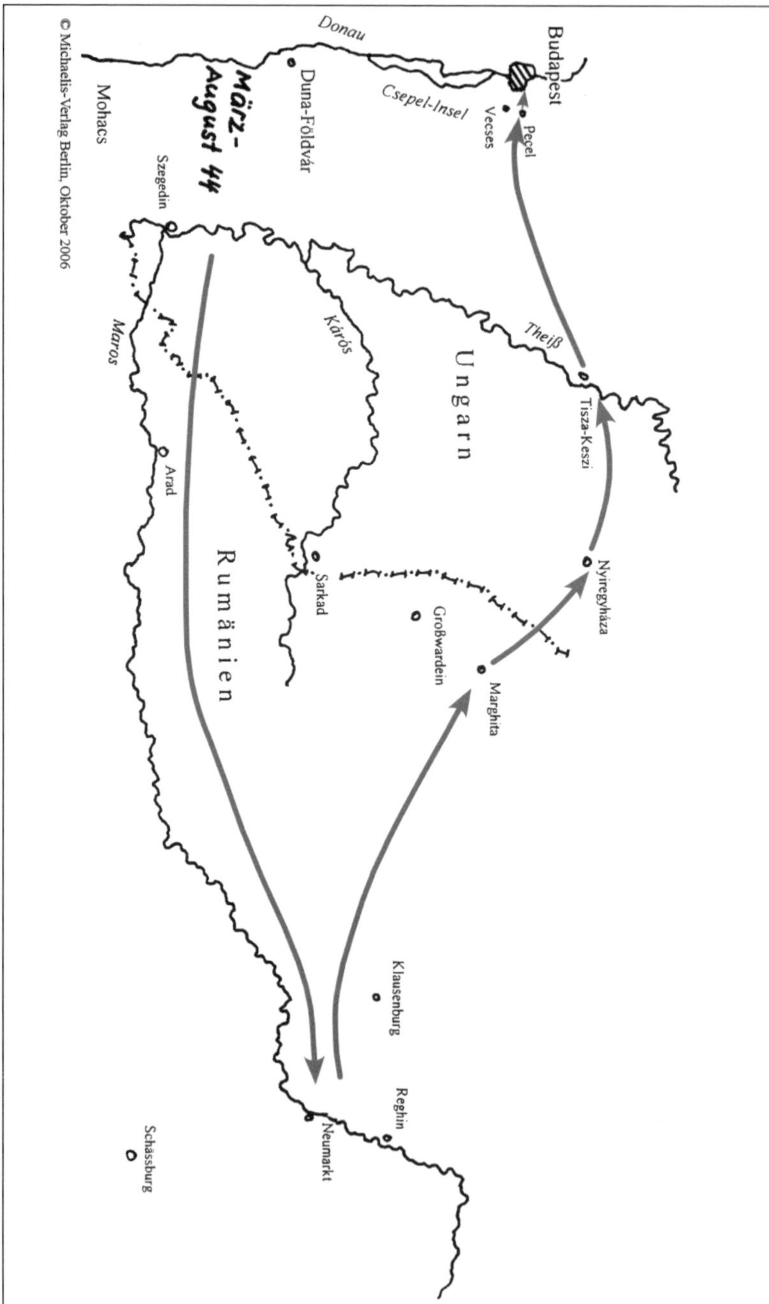
Budapest
Donau
Csepel-Insel
Vecses
Peçel
Duna-Földvár
März-
August 44
Mohacs
Szegedin
Theiß
Ungarn
Körös
Maros
Tisza-Keszi
Arad
Nyiregyháza
Sarkad
Großwardein
Rumänien
Marghita
Klausenburg
Reghin
Neumarkt
Schässburg
© Michaelis-Verlag Berlin, Oktober 2006

Division "Feldherrnhalle," began moving into the Pestszentlörinc area (approximately 3.7 miles southeast of Budapest), where they occupied the line Vecses–Üllö–Peczel. The latter villages were part of the Karola Position, which followed the line Vecses–Gyömrö–Maglod–Peczel. This was supposed to form the Hungarian capital's outer defense belt. Construction of the line had only begun in November 1944, and it was not a proper defense line with bunkers and prepared positions.

While the frequent formation and dissolution of battle groups caused the units to become increasingly mixed, at the end of November 1944, Headquarters, *IX. Waffen-Gebirgs-Korps der SS* arrived in Budapest from the Balkans and on December 13, assumed command of III Panzer Corps. Just four days earlier the first Soviet battalions had crossed the Danube and established a bridgehead about 18.5 miles south of the capital.

After several quiet days, Budapest was encircled by Soviet troops at Christmas 1944. The units of the cavalry divisions were still on the eastern bank of the Danube (Pest) at that time, holding bridgeheads with units of the *Wehrmacht*. On December 25, 1944, the 8th SS Cavalry Division received orders to withdraw from the eastern bridgehead in order to, with units of the *Panzergrenadier-Division "Feldherrnhalle,"* prevent the Soviets from entering the strategically more important western part of the city (Buda).

When Soviet tanks advanced from Bia (approximately ten miles west of Budapest) toward Budakeszi, 8.7 miles away, the 8th SS Armored Reconnaissance Battalion was deployed to screen Budaörs (approximately five miles west of Budapest) and secure Budakeszi.

Northwest of Csepel, enemy units crossed the Budapest to Budaörs rail line and from Budafok Soviet troops crossed to Csepel Island. The German and Hungarian defenders were subsequently forced to give up Vecses, Maglod, Pestszentlörinc and Rakoscsaba. In temperatures of minus ten degrees there was fierce house fighting near Budakeszi. On December 29, 1944, Soviet marshalls Malinovsky and Tolbukhin called on the defenders to surrender, but in vain. They then gave the garrison of Budapest an ultimatum.

Even as Budapest was being encircled, the German command was planning to relieve the Hungarian capital. Given the relationship of forces that existed, this was an almost hopeless undertaking.

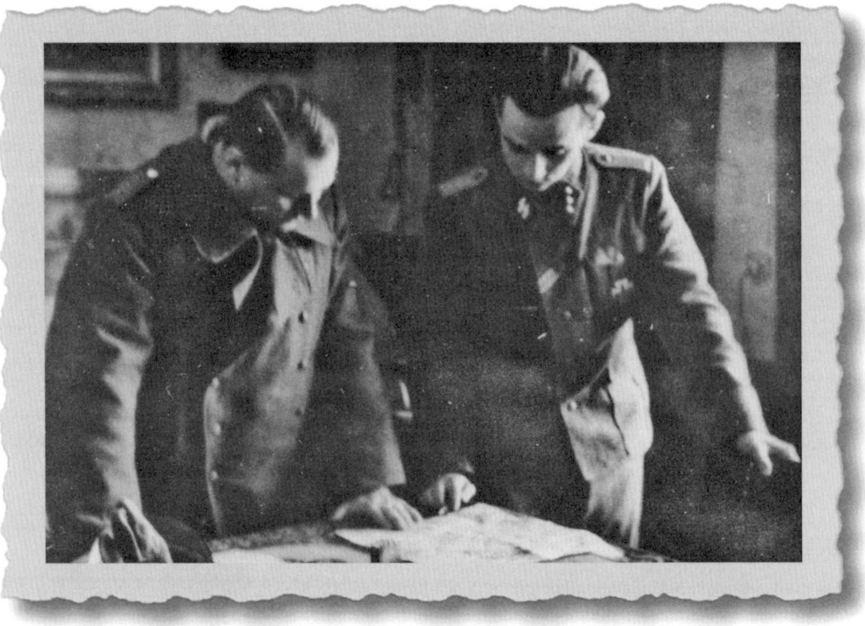

The last commander of the 8th SS Cavalry Division "Florian Geyer," *SS-Oberführer* Joachim Rumohr.

Nevertheless, on December 31, 1944, the IV SS Panzer Corps attacked towards Budapest, where there were almost 6,000 wounded. The medical care system had broken down and the men were subsisting on one slice of bread per day.

By January 13, 1945, the 10th SS Panzergrenadier Regiment "Westland" of the 5th SS Panzer Division "Wiking" had advanced as far as Pilisszentkereszt. Then Hitler ordered the relief force to halt. The attempt to liberate Budapest, which was close to being realized, had to be broken off.

The next day the *IX. Waffen-Gebirgs-Korps der SS* reported that it had expended its artillery ammunition and that small arms ammunition and fuel were running out. As a result, its remaining guns and tanks could not be used and had to be blown up by their users.

On January 16, 1945, the eastern bridgehead was still present from the area Franz-Joseph Bridge–Calvin Square–Elizabeth Ring–Baro Street to the Danube. Margaret Island formed its northern tip. The next day, the eastern bridgehead was evacuated, and on January 18, 1945, the last intact bridges were blown. The 8th SS Armored Reconnaissance Battalion took up positions on the west bank of the Danube at the Margaret Bridge and was able to determine that the Hungarians had erected barricades from sacks of flour!

Also on that day the IV SS Panzer Corps launched another relief effort—this time from the southwest. After initial success, the attack had to be halted on January 27, 1945.

Hungarian units went over to the Red Army and were immediately sent into action against German units. On January 29, *IX. Waffen-Gebirgs-Korps der SS* reported that the number of wounded already outnumbered those still fighting. The combat zone had meanwhile shrunk to Gellért Hill and the castle. Wounded soldiers and civilians stayed in the numerous underground passageways.

At the beginning of February 1945, fierce street and house fighting again broke out. The by then approximately 11,000 wounded could only be given fifteen grams of lentils and half a slice of bread and there were only sufficient stocks remaining for two days of even this quantity.

On February 8, 1945, the last guns of the 8th SS Flak Battalion shot down their seventy-fifth confirmed enemy aircraft. In recent days the still intact guns for which there was no ammunition were placed on the university grounds on the castle hill, while the gunners fought as infantry.

On February 8, 1945, Hitler rejected a request from *IX. Waffen-Gebirgs-Korps der SS* for permission to break out because it would have failed anyway and at least Fortress Budapest was serving a purpose in tying down powerful enemy forces. The next day the enemy took Gellért Hill, after which the only remaining resistance was on the castle hill and the citadel.

On Sunday February 11, 1945, *SS-Obergruppenführer* Pfeffer-Wildenbruch informed the OKW by radio that the Soviets were about to split the small pocket and that holding out further could only result in unconditional surrender or destruction. He subsequently decided on his own authority to break out.

Covered by the remnants of the 22nd SS Volunteer Cavalry Division, what was left of the 8th SS Cavalry Division and the 13th Panzer Division would break out to the west and northwest (Szomor–Mariahalom or Pilis Mountains–Piliszentlelek). A fourth group was to attempt to escape through the underground sewer system. In preparation for the breakout, which was to begin at 2000, the troops gathered in the castle. There the last rations were given out, after which the troops moved into their starting positions. Despite the secrecy the Red Army learned the exact time of the breakout. At 2000 Soviet artillery began pounding the castle. Within a short time the streets were covered with fallen and wounded.

On February 15, 1945, the *Wehrmacht* communiqué reported: "After the complete encirclement of Budapest, the defenders held the city for almost fifty days against fierce enemy attacks and tied down far superior Soviet forces. Now, with ammunition and food running out, the courageous German and Hungarian garrison has been ordered to break through the siege ring. The first elements have already reached our front west of Budapest."

The first and subsequent elements totaled 785 men from approximately eight divisions! Beginning February 14, 1945, they reached the German prepared positions in the Zsambek (approximately 15.5 miles west of Budapest) area. Most of the troops were killed during the dramatic breakout or were taken prisoner by the Soviets. The approximately 100 survivors of the 8th SS Cavalry Division, together with the survivors from the 22nd SS Volunteer Cavalry Division, were subsequently integrated into the 37th SS Volunteer Cavalry Division, which was in the formation process.

The total losses for the *8th SS Cavalry Division "Florian Geyer"* since July 22, 1941 were:

Killed: 110 officers and 3,063 other ranks
Wounded: 222 officers and 9,381 other ranks
Missing: 19 officers and 1,098 other ranks

The division had thus suffered losses almost equal to its entire authorized personnel strength. Formed and equipped for use in the rear area, the SS Cavalry Brigade and later the SS Cavalry Division were repeatedly ordered to the front as the last reserve and initially were able to help stabilize the situation. When, in 1943, the Red Army's materiel superiority became too great, the division was completely smashed at the front southwest of Kharkov. Drawing the necessary conclusions from this situation, in early 1944 an attempt was made to turn the unit into a division capable of being used at the front by adding motorized heavy supporting units—such as a motorized artillery battalion, for example. A successful deployment in Transylvania was prevented by the materiel superiority of the Soviet forces and the weakness of the German–Hungarian units. In the end, after the loss of all their heavy weapons and vehicles, the units were destroyed in a purely infantry action in Budapest in February 1945. For their actions in the rear area against partisans and civilians, the members of the division captured by the Soviets received the most severe punishment and the majority did not return from the USSR until 1955–56.

Appendix 2: The SS Cavalry Training and Replacement Regiment

SS Cavalry Replacement Battalion

When the *SS-Totenkopf-Reiterstandarte* were formed in September 1939, a replacement troop was initially formed in Munich. After the *Standarte* (regiment) was transferred to the Generalgouvernement, the troop followed to Warsaw.

When orders were given for the formation of the SS Cavalry Brigade in the spring of 1941, the replacement troop provided the core for the SS Cavalry Replacement Battalion with three cavalry troops, a heavy troop and a bicycle training troop.

Beginning April 19, 1943, the battalion, with a strength of ten officers and 450 other ranks, took part in the clearing of the Warsaw ghetto under the command of *SS-Brigadeführer* Stroop, the SS and Police Commander in the Warsaw District. In the action, which lasted until May 16, 1943, 56,000 Jews were deported, mainly to Lublin and Auschwitz. One member of the SS Cavalry Replacement Battalion was killed, and 29 were wounded.

Effective October 22, 1943, the unit was renamed the 8th SS Cavalry Training and Replacement Battalion. Because of the Soviet advance through the Generalgouvernement to the gates of Warsaw, in July 1944 the battalion was transferred to SS Training Camp Böhmen. From August 1, 1944, the battalion headquarters and a cleanup detachment of about 100 men helped put down the Warsaw uprising.

SS Cavalry Training and Replacement Regiment

After the formation of the 22nd SS Volunteer Cavalry Division began in early May 1944, effective August 15, 1944, the training and replacement battalion was expanded into the SS Cavalry Training and Replacement Regiment.

When the Red Army advanced to the Oder in January 1945, the regiment was placed on alert and received orders to form a battle group. A battalion-strength battle group was formed under the command of the regimental commander, *SS-Obersturmbannführer* Plänk and attached to XXXXVIII Army Corps (17th Army).

Ordered to the Waldenburg area south of Striegaus in Silesia (approximately thirty-one miles southwest of Breslau), SS-Battle Group Plänk was not employed directly in the front, instead moving into a line of security in the rear. After the end of the so-called Silesian Operation by the Soviets at the end of February 1945, the SS cavalry were transferred back to SS Training Camp Böhmen.

On May 5, 1945, an uprising began in Prague with Czech resistance fighters and German troops battling for the radio station building. Czech flags were raised in many places in the city and barricades erected. As the day went on, rebels occupied important German administration buildings and attacked and in some cases disarmed German units. Prior to this individuals had been attacked. The Czech troops gained control of about half the city and encircled other German strongpoints. German units outside the city were alerted and began securing the main transport and communications links inside the city. Their goal was to cover the departure of the German population and military units from the city to the west.

After just a few hours the German forces had the situation under control again. Intent on making an example, the commander of the *Waffen-SS* in Bohemia and Moravia, *SS-Gruppenführer und Generalleutnant der Waffen-SS* Carl Friedrich von Pückler-Burghauss, ordered that the inner city of Prague be blown up, as had been done in Warsaw three-quarters of a year before.

After no Allied help arrived and the city was being destroyed, the rebels decided to open negotiations with the German commander in the Military District of Bohemia and Moravia, *General der Infanterie* Rudolf Toussaint. A ceasefire was agreed upon, assuring German troops and civilians free exit from the city, while on the other side the German forces were to halt the destruction of the city.

SS Battle Group Plänk was stopped by Czech rebels while on its way to Prague. Finally, the SS cavalry proceeded on foot towards Kunratice—a suburb of Prague—and moved into assembly areas there. At about noon on May 7, 1945, the battle group began advancing along the main road to Prague. They came under fire and what followed was costly street and house fighting. After taking heavy casualties the units withdrew to their starting positions. A fresh advance on Prague was supposed to take place the next day, but this was called off on account of the German surrender. Instead resistance was to be offered until the German civilian population had been evacuated. After this the troops attempted—for the most part without success—to surrender to the Americans. As a rule, those that were taken prisoner by the Americans were satisfactory turned over to the Czechs or Soviets.

Other Schiffer Books by Rolf Michaelis

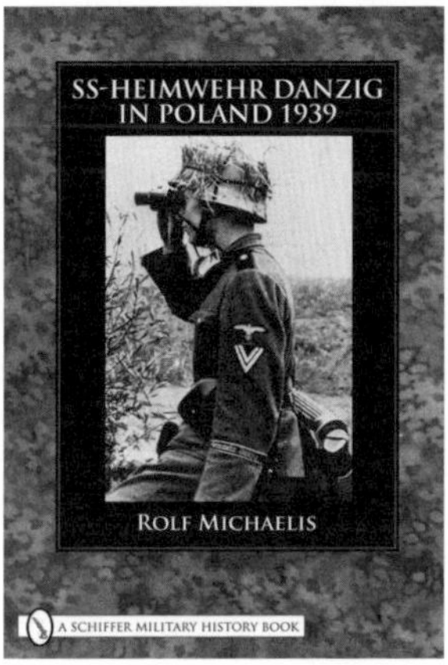

SS-Heimwehr Danzig
in Poland, 1939
(978-0-7643-2943-2)

Panzer Divisions
of the Waffen-SS
(978-0-7643-4477-0)

SS-Fallschirmjäger-Bataillon 500/600
(978-0-7643-2944-9)

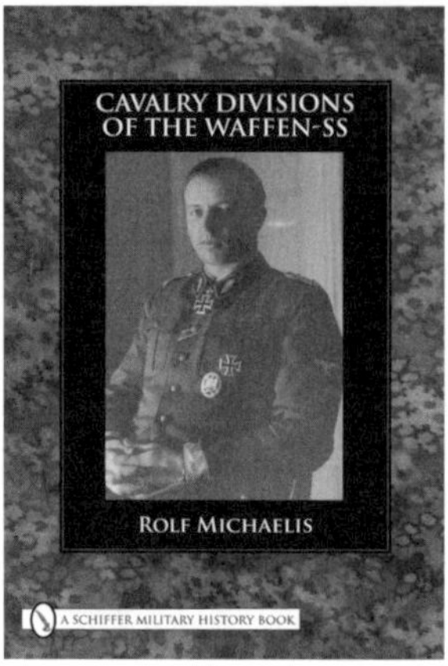

Cavalry Divisions
of the Waffen-SS
(978-0-7643-3661-4)

The SS-Sonderkommando
"Dirlewanger"
(978-0-7643-4479-4)

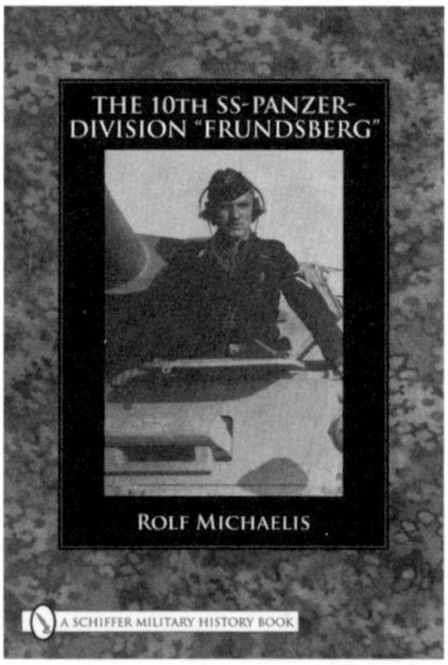

The 10th SS-Panzer-Division "Frundsberg"
(978-0-7643-3099-5)

Estonians in the Waffen-SS
(978-0-7643-3350-7)

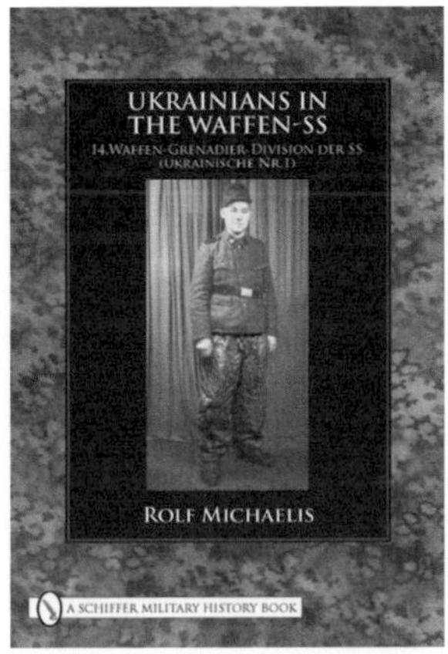

Ukrainians in the Waffen-SS
(978-0-7643-3349-1)

Belgians in the Waffen-SS
(978-0-7643-4034-5)

Other Schiffer Books on Related Subjects

Cavalry of the Wehrmacht by Klaus Richter
(0-88740-814-1)

Horses of the German Army in WWII by Paul Johnson
(0-7643-2421-7)

Other Schiffer Books in this Series

Leo Wilm's Memories of the Waffen-SS
(978-0-7643-5298-0)